Dad, how do I get rich?

1st edition

Written by

Dr. Michael Görgen

Imprint

Text
Copyright © 2023 Michael Görgen

Editing
Jenn Morril

Cover design
Dr. Simon Görgen

All rights reserved.
ISBN: 9798850320225

For my sons Márcio and Benicio: to give you that all-important 500-meter head start in the marathon of life

Table of Contents

Why this book? 8

Preface for parents 10

How I get rich as a child 13

    What do you need money for? 13

    So why is money important today? 17

    Why do people want more money? 19

    What does being rich mean to you? 27

Dad, how do I get rich? 31

    Saving - Start early and get rich faster! 31

    Investing - how you get more with less! 44

    These investments exist! 48

        The bank 48

        The principle of supply and demand 55

        The stock market 58

This is how I get rich, Dad! 64

    My steps to wealth 64

    The magic for my wealth 68

Timetable of getting rich 71

On the way to wealth, you must not forget 76

Final word for you 78

Introduction for parents: How to use this book effectively 80

    For all parents of rich children 83

    What can you do for your rich child! 85

    The power of the compound effect 91

    Saving recommendation for the parents of rich children 96

    Excursus: Exchange Traded Funds – ETFs 98

    Stock valuation and investment strategies 101

    The additional booster to get rich! 104

    Conclusion for parents of rich kids 108

Appendix 111

    Word Explanations 111

    Book recommendations 115

    Summary of the book 117

    What do you need money for? 118

    So why is money important today? 119

    Why do people want more money? 119

    What does being rich mean to you? 120

    Saving - Start early and get rich faster! 121

    Investments - how to get more with less! 124

    These investments exist 126

- Investments in products: Supply and demand 129
- My steps to wealth 131
- The magic for my wealth 134
- Timeplan of getting rich 135
- Introduction for Parents: How to use the book effectively 136
  - What can you do for your rich child!? 138
  - The power of the compound effect 141
- My excellence diary 142

Why this book?

How many kids and teens do you know who know anything about banks, stock markets, or investing? Perhaps your experience is the same as mine, and it's only a handful among the thousands that I've met on my own path or through the agency of my sons.

What's more, how many of those kids have stock portfolios, a savings plan or a concrete monthly savings goal when they are ten, twelve or 15 years old, and a few years later have already saved a few thousand euros?

The subject of finance is not a subject in the classroom because, according to the Ministry of Education, it has no relevance in a child's education. It is left up to everyone individually to acquire the knowledge for themselves as an adult, if they ever acquire it at all. However, practice shows that this happens quite rarely. There are far too many adults with money problems, private insolvencies and old-age poverty or people who, despite a good income, struggle with a constant lack of money! That leads us to ask whether this is connected with the fact that the possibilities for investing money were simply never learned.

Everyone has a relationship with finances, whether voluntarily or involuntarily. This may also be the case with school subjects such as art, chemistry, or philosophy, but usually a large part of private success in life is not linked to such subjects. Why isn't the foundation for knowledge of money and finance, just as with many other school subjects, laid down in childhood? It would make so much sense!

This book fills this obvious gap in the education of children and young people. What's more, in addition to sound, child-friendly technical knowledge combined with vivid short stories, you'll also find concrete recommendations for action on how best to save money. And a timetable for getting rich.

With the knowledge in this book, every child can learn to become rich in a fun and playful way. This learning is supported by short, catchy exercises. The book is divided into two chapters:

> "How to get rich as a child!"
>
> "For all parents of rich children".

Preface for parents

This is not a parenting guidebook. It is a guidebook about money. And yet, especially in childhood, knowledge and the handling of money are shaped through a child's upbringing. Therefore, I need you as parents, to be involved in teaching your child about money. I have two children myself and know how individual education is from family to family, even within the family from child to child. It takes a lot of sensitivity to always strike the right note, especially when it comes to teaching financial literacy. For this to succeed, we have to work well together - that is what I request of you.

This book is a compilation of financial ideas, investment concepts, experiences, and thought-provoking ideas that you can use to support your educational philosophy. In doing so, I will primarily show (in a child-friendly way) which mechanisms work for adults and are easy to apply at any age. Of course, I will always recommend specific things that can be done but just check what might suit your child best. I will show you concrete methods that anyone can use to create a budget for investing by taking small, simple steps to save. With this budget, you and your child can then start getting rich.

When I was 26 and finally discovered the wonder of the stock market, stocks and ETFs, real estate, and "professional" targeted saving, my finances literally went through the roof. I've always been good at math. You'll see, though, that being math affine is not necessary. Everyone can - if they want to - quickly understand the logic behind processes such as interest-interest or returns.

Because I had much richer friends who could afford great vacations and the latest cell phone every year, I had a strong drive to become rich myself. That's why saving came easily to me. By the time I was 30, my wife and I already owned two apartments, a stock portfolio with a large, five-figure sum and a high, six-figure amount in "cash". With that, we were able to fulfill our dream of owning our own home. Granted, we both had good jobs and worked hard, but had never put anything aside before. Our "investment strategy" until then consisted of buying the latest fashion, the best shoes and two expensive vacations per year.

By the way, I have absolutely nothing to do with money management professionally. I simply enjoy taking advantage of all the opportunities that present themselves to those people who delve deeper into the subject. This has developed into a wealth of knowledge that I would like to pass on to my own sons, to you, and your children. Think of it as a hobby - but one that I am quite proficient in. In my main profession I am an engineer.

Today I mourn the missed opportunities of my 20s: Why was it that I started investing so late? As Robert Kyosaki, one of my favorite authors, says, "One of the wonders of mankind is interest-interest." If I had invested €25 every month in ETFs with a moderate growth rate of 6% ten years earlier, at 16, I would have had a good starting capital for further investments of almost €4,000 at 26, or over €10,000 ten years later. Admittedly, €25 per month is a lot of money for a 16-year-old on the one hand, but on the other hand you have other goals at this age than to have money in your account ten years later. That's where you as parents come in: either as financiers or at least as good role models in terms of consumer behavior.

So, we're talking about two target groups, so to speak: children and parents. That's why this book is divided into two parts: The first part, for all parents - focuses on what you can do as a supporter, backer or with (small) amounts of money to make it easier for your child to become rich. The other part is specially designed for children and introduces them to the topics of money, saving and investing with small, memorable stories. In this way, children are motivated to save money themselves, or even to invest it - together with their parents. You will see that you don't need mathematics to invest, only motivation and goals. I will also support you and your child in this endeavor.

One of the primary reasons I wrote this book: to make it easy for my children and yours to save money at an early age, so that they don't have to mourn missed opportunities when they're 30. This way, they can tap their full "get-rich-quick" potential as early as possible.

And everything I say here of course always applies to boys as well as girls, to men as well as women!

I wish everyone every success in getting rich!

Yours

Michael Görgen

How I get rich as a child

What do you need money for?

Do you remember standing in the toy aisle and dreaming of having the new Barbie, the new Lego, the coolest racing car or a trendy board game? But, your parents didn't want to buy it for you and you didn't have enough pocket money? How did you feel then? Were you sad? Angry or disappointed?

This book exists to ensure that this feeling doesn't rule your life and you don't still have to think as an adult: "What a bummer! It's not enough! It's never enough!", Yes, having money is important! So are health, happiness and contentment of course, (more on that later, at the end of the book). I would like to explain in the following chapter why money is generally so important to people.

What money actually is ...

Money is, above all, a means of feeling secure and a method of not to having money worries. Thus, it can help us in not being unhappy. But money alone does not make a person happy. There are many other things involved in happiness including love and health.

Money has been around for more than 2,000 years. This has

What do you need money for?

been shown by excavations of ancient cities. At that time, money was still made of gold or silver. For a long time, however, it was also possible to exchange goods - for example, grain for meat or new shoes for a new coat. And that was despite the fact that money, for example in the form of coins, already existed.

If you or I had gone to a real medieval market 500 years ago to buy a kilo of bread, we would most likely have had to barter for it. Anything the seller wanted could be considered "currency" because often, the seller simply didn't have it. Or, seller could not afford it. For example, if they had neither eggs nor meat, because they had only a field for grain, but no stable for animals ... or, if they were in need of labor because his own time was not enough. Such a purchase was then become an agreement among people and it would be agreed that 20 eggs were equal in value to one kilo of bread.

Now imagine that we would like to buy something bigger than a kilo of bread, say a horse to aid our work in the fields. We would have had to bring very, very, very many eggs to offer the equivalent of the horse and close the deal. We could, of course, trade the horse for three pigs. But what if the seller didn't want any pigs at all? Then our deal would not go through.

♠Intermediate Conclusion♠

So you see, without money, shopping would either be very costly (bringing lots of eggs to trade) or not possible at all (if our barter goods are not needed or wanted).

Money solves both the drawback of unnecessary quantity and/or unwanted goods because it is very small and provides a convenience. A 100 Euro bill weighs 1.02 grams, an egg weighs at least 50 times as much, depending on its size, and is worth only $1/200^{th}$. If an egg costs 50 cents, the difference in weight between the egg and the 100 Euro bill is about a factor of 10,000 for the same value!

In addition, money is much more comprehensively valid. To remain with our example from above, the dealer could buy the horse that they want with money. Of course, they could also buy three pigs with it. But they would not have to take the pigs we brought. If it is not a barter, he can decide for himself if and how many pigs are wanted.

What do you need money for?

🎵 Summarized 🎵

Money is a means to an end and facilitates the trading of goods, food, or greater things. It is its own agreement, so it is a different way of trading than bartering.

So why is money important today?

We're back in the same year as the last chapter, about 500 years ago. Imagine your parents have a small garden, two chickens and a goat. The garden provides you with vegetables and fruit, you get eggs from the chickens and milk or meat from the goat. You have almost everything you need to live. The rest you exchange: with your neighbors, traders or other people you know. Your parents sew their clothes themselves. They use their labor to do the daily work in the fields, thus directly ensuring your survival.

Today, in the 21st century, hardly anyone has gardens large enough to live on. Unless your parents are farmers, but then they will sell the harvest rather than use the produce themselves.

Your parents may earn money by working as craftsmen or repair other people's things for money. Perhaps they are teachers and teach children or they are self-employed and get paid directly by customers. Or maybe they offer their labor to a company and get money for it. Whatever it may be, with the proceeds of their labor or "money" they can buy bread, eggs or anything else from others who are able to agree on the value of that money.

Did you know?

Only two percent of the German population are farmers. What does that mean? First and foremost, that a lot has changed since the Middle Ages: After all, the average person could hardly provide for ourselves anymore. With a population of over 80 million, it would be impossible for

So why is money important today?

everyone in Germany to have enough land to provide for themselves on a permanent basis. What, for example, does the family that lives in the high-rise in "Berlin-Mitte" do? Where would their piece of land be? Besides, 15 % of of the land in Germany is built up with all kinds of things: Train stations, roads, highways and, of course, houses). And 30 % is forest All this is not directly usable as arable land.

!That means!

Today you can buy things with money. Your parents don't use their labor to grow fruits or vegetables to feed themselves and you. That is hardly possible anymore. Instead, they offer their labor to a company and get money for it.

Why do people want more money?

If every adult would only buy food from their earned money, surely everyone would manage well with their salary and would not have to earn more and more. But nearly everybody wants more than just that. They want a bigger apartment, a faster car, nicer clothes, a new cell phone ...

You probably recognize this condition. You think those shoes are great, or you're dying to have the latest iPhone. The desire for the newest and best things increases when your friends or siblings have something you don't have. That's usually called envy. Then there's: When other people buy what you have, they become "copycats", and you have the feeling that that really sucks. At least that's how it always was with me and my older brother. He never wanted me to get the same shoes as him to avoid that dilemma. It made him lose the feeling of being unique, even though I'm sure that wasn't clear to my brother as a child.

This striving for more (more money, more cars, more toys) and uniqueness is deeply rooted in all people. But has it always been this way, or has it only developed in modern times?

Let's go back in time about 4,500 years to the Pharoah's Egypt and look at their pyramids. They are spectacular, but nothing more than tombs. You might wonder if anyone needs such a house as their final resting place that, at over 130 meters, is taller and larger than many skyscrapers today? We can likely agree that people certainly do not require such resting places but it does show us the engrained human desire to leave something for eternity, or perhaps to show

Why do people want more money?

that one is better, grander, or more important than others. The gigantic buildings are a demonstration of power. Everyone living at that time was meant to clearly see and understand the superiority of the Egyptian rulers.

Today we define superiority or uniqueness not by pyramids, but for example by fancy and expensive clothes, colorful hair or simply by behaving differently than the "broad masses". If this behavior of wanting to be better than others existed 4,500 years ago, could it be assumed that it has always existed?

The answer is: yes! Just think of the animals. Surely you have seen the courtship behavior of birds, that is, the courtship of the male bird to find a female bird. This is often done by singing loudly and beautifully. Or with a beautiful plumage tries to convince the partner of his health and stature as a potential mate. It is important for male birds to sing more beautifully, to have more beautiful feathers or to "dance" more wonderfully than all the other males. Then the female can select the suitor. Seen in this way, it is "essential for survival" at least for the respective male bird to be better than all the others. Because only having won this contest is the male chosen for reproduction and thus ensuring the survival of its genes.

In this way, nature created a natural and extremely strong will in its creatures with the goal of being better than others at the center of success. Succeeding ensures the survival of the respective kind by reproduction and passing on of the genes. This behavior is, in modified form, is transferable to all living beings. Other animals even fight for females, this is an even more obvious competition for dominance.

Why do people want more money?

The first humans, you may have heard in school, evolved about 200,000 years ago. Since we are descended from apes, which have been around for 30 million years and thus much longer than us, we share many genes with them. As a result, large parts of our brain are significantly older than humans. This is because we have virtually "inherited" many parts of our brain. With this inheritance, we have primarily adopted instincts and behavior patterns that ensured our survival 200,000 years ago. Back then, when we had to fight for our lives every day as one "animal" among many.

Even if 200,000 years probably seem like a very long time to you: For our development, it's rather short. And today, in the 21st century, we still have almost all the instincts from our ancestors. We are often not even aware of these instincts, and most of them are no longer absolutely necessary for survival. Unfortunately, we cannot simply turn them on or off, but rather we must live with them and cope with them.

Of course, we have developed significantly in some things in comparison to our animal ancestors. Many things would be completely foreign to animals, such as finances. And the desire to be significant, as in the example with the pyramids, is what most distinguishes us from animals. No animal does things to be significant. In nature, all serves a recreational goal. This means that we humans have not only inherited the desire to be better than others from our ancestors, but this desire has even increased over time. Now we even want to be significant. And all this is reflected in today's world, especially in the desire for more money!

♥To become rich...

Because of the desire to be better than

Why do people want more money?

others, most people want to become rich! This is a strong drive. For you too?

For this statement, I brought a little exercise for you to think about what drives you and what you need money for.

Exercise:

What do you need money for?

1.
2.
3.

What have you ever bought that you needed to save up for?

1.
2.
3.

What would you buy with a whole lot of money?

1.
2.
3.

In the exercises, I really care about:

►The exercises◄

Please don't skip the exercises! No one has ever gotten rich from just reading. What's important is that you internalize what you read, and the easiest way to do that is through these short exercises. You can always return to the exercises if something occurs to you in between ... Ask your parents what they would write here!

They say a picture is worth a thousand words. You may have heard this saying before. It's said mainly because the brain works best with pictures and can memorize them better than just words in a book. Because that's the case, there's a great technique from personal development (I give you great reading tips on this in the appendix of the book, for example by Tony Robbins).

The technique I'm referring to here is called a "vision board." The result is a piece of cardboard or paper on which you depict all your goals, dreams and desires. I recommend this technique also to you, because with it you will always have your goals in front of your eyes. You can download pictures from the internet, print them out and glue them in or paint something you want to own or achieve. For example, I

Why do people want more money?

downloaded an old Porsche as a photo and pasted it in, as well as a picture of a pool, because it is my dream to own a vacation home by the sea with its own pool.

The really great thing about the Vision Board is that you can put together your own wishes and look at them over and over again - preferably every day. I have reserved the next two pages for this vision board where you can paste or draw pictures. That way you can always flip back to that spot.

Why do people want more money?

This is the vision board from:

Created on:
Revised on:

What does being rich mean to you?

"Being rich" is primarily a matter of opinion, almost a feeling. Just as everyone answers the question "what do you have to laugh about?" differently, everyone answers the question "what does being rich actually mean?" differently.

I have been fortunate to have traveled a lot and, on my travels, I have been able to become acquainted with various countries and cultures and have especially enjoyed connecting with the people in the countries I traveled to. I also liked to use those opportunities of meeting new people to talk about personal idea of how, for example, various cultures respond to the question of what being rich means from their cultural perspective. I've will share some of those different perspectives for you here:

Hernandinho, 21 years old, Cape Verde, Africa says:

"For me, being rich means being able to do what I want. At the same time, I want to be unconstrained. We don't have a lot of money, but I have exactly what I need here in Cape Verde and I feel blessed, or in other words, rich."

Niklas, 7 years old, Germany, Europe, told me the following about the question:

"If I were rich, I would buy as many toys as I can and my parents a bigger house. I have to share a room with my sister Liliana. I think that's stupid."

What does being rich mean to you?

Scott, 43, England, Europe, told me:

"I actually have everything I want. If I had a lot more money, I would donate most of it and do something good. I would probably build a school in one of the many countries where there are still no schools for children. But I also think a Porsche is good and would maybe buy one."

Noemia, 55, Angola, Africa:

"I am healthy, my family is healthy, I am rich".

Pooja, 14, India, Asia, a colleagues sister told me in a WhatsApp phone call:

"I know my family doesn't have much money. But I get to go to school every day, so I am richer than many other children in India."

•Conclusion•

You can see from the variance in answers that, "being rich" can refer to many things- not just money. To some it might mean things that are harder to value such as happiness and health. In the chapters, however, we will focus on money and everything that can be grasped with the hands when we talk about being rich. Of course, we won't forget happiness and health.

So being rich seems to mean very different things to different people. Often people use the word rich in the context of having something in abundance (money, toys). It can be said that a family is "child-rich" if it has many children. For adults, being rich also means independence, as many vacations as possible, numerous trips, not having to work anymore, or having so much money that you can also donate it to people who are not making ends meet.

What does being rich mean to you?

Exercise:

What does being rich mean to you?

1.
2.
3.

What would you like to have if everything were free?

1.
2.
3.

To whom would you give something? What would you give to that person?

1.
2.
3.

Dad, how do I get rich?

In this chapter, I will introduce you to the steps on how to become rich. There is always a short story with explanations and exercises.

Saving - Start early and get rich faster!

Marie is a smart and careful girl. When her father brings in the potato harvest in the fall, she is just as happy as her brothers about the big, yellow potatoes. Her mouth is already watering at the thought of Mama's potatoes with meat in gravy. This year's harvest was very big.

Her father is totally over the moon and invites the neighbors to a Thanksgiving feast. When her father also slaughters a pig out of sheer joy to celebrate, Marie thinks back to the harsh winter of five years ago. That year, her family almost starved to death. Now it seems like a waste to Marie to slaughter a pig "just like that."

Marie lives in 1723, supermarkets don't exist, only small food markets that are completely overpriced. At least that's what Mama says. That's why her family has to live on, almost exclusively, what they can produce for themselves.

Saving - Start early and get rich faster!

In the evening, the harvest festival takes place, all of the neighbors are invited to the celebration. Late at night, when all the adults are asleep and snoring loudly because they have drunk too much beer, Marie sneaks into the barn with her youngest brother Christian. Their plan is simple: move a few potatoes aside and use them to set up a secret camp. In case times get tough again. Both children think this is necessary. Because father literally lives "from hand to mouth." He is not at all good at saving, neither food nor money, which is always tight anyway. Marie is 14 years old, and she will never forget the terrible feeling of hunger when there were only very, very small rations to eat.

The next day, when the adults wake up, almost ten percent of the potatoes are gone. That is, every tenth potato. That's a lot and a nightmare for Marie's father. Marie and Christian secretly took them to their ally, Grandma Sofie. It was a lot of work, though, since Marie and Christian couldn't carry that many heavy sacks of potatoes at once. But with Dad's wheelbarrow, they finally made it. Since Grandma Sofie knows that Marie's father is bad at planning ahead, she gladly made her old cellar available. No one ever goes down there because Sofie no longer stores her food there. The constant stair climbing has become too much for her.

While the tree leaves change color from gold to dark brown, the temperatures are already dropping. And before Marie knows it, it has snowed. When she gets up to help her mother with her sewing and embroidery, the world has covered itself with a thin, white layer of snow. Marie's father is harvesting the last of the winter vegetables, filling the storehouses as much as he can. It's Christmas and once again there's a big, debauched feast. There is so much food ready that the small

Saving - Start early and get rich faster!

table in the cozy living room almost bends. Marie watches it all from her position next to the stove. It is wonderfully warm there. She is looking forward to Christmas, the great food and the beautiful songs by the stove. Yet she wonders, "Who's going to eat all of this?"

And indeed, just like last year, there is a lot of food left over. Some of it the family eats on the days after Christmas, which is not bad either. The rest they feed to the chickens and goats. What a waste!

In February, when the temperatures are still far below freezing and the small village pond is still frozen over, Marie's mom's kitchen doesn't really get warm either. Not only the firewood is saved, but also the food. Again ... Because the supplies are running out. The family tightens its belt and eats less and less. The cold lasts unusually long this year, and by now it is piercing the family's marrow.

In mid-March, father brings the last carrots and potatoes into the house; meat has been gone for three weeks. The next day, father asks the neighbors for help, but they have to stock up on their own so as not to get into the same situation as Marie's family. Grandma Sofie can't help either. She has some food left over, but that's not enough to feed a family of six. (Yes, Marie has two other siblings besides Christian).

Marie waits three days, during which the family lives on nothing but stale, stale bread. Then she decides that Father should have learned his lesson and sneaks off to Grandma Sofie's at night, accompanied by Christian.

When father goes to the barn the next morning, he is astonished: 20 kilos of potatoes are piled up there, innocently

Saving - Start early and get rich faster!

waiting to be stuffed into hungry mouths. That's enough for at least two weeks. Father falls to his knees and thanks God for this miracle. Marie watches him from a distance with a sly smile and is pleased.

▶ What have you learned?

1. Saving is especially important when you are doing well. However, saving does not always refer only to money, as we have seen. It is also possible to save food.
2. It's important to plan ahead. This was not only true in 1723, it remains true today.
3. You must not waste anything, neither food nor money. Otherwise, it will take its revenge at some point.

What does that mean for us now in the 21st century? What does saving mean today?

Do you know this? Your aunt gives you 20 € after a visit. And says, "Buy yourself something nice with it ..." Then you go and buy "something nice" for 20 €. This is basically not very different from the way Marie's father behaved: always spending or consuming everything right away, as soon as he got it, never saving anything. Only, hopefully, you'll never have to go hungry.

Saving - Start early and get rich faster!

If you too run to the nearest store to buy "something nice" as soon as you have money in your hand, you are not alone in this. It is a behavior that is typical for humans. Many people find it difficult to plan for a distant future and prefer to live in the here and now. The reason for this behavior used to make a lot of sense. For example, if you imagine elephants, giraffes or lions in the savannah, these animals are always looking for the next food, a way to drink water or they are looking for shelter. They literally live from paw to mouth and don't have to plan much more than a few days in advance.

The first humans, as we learned earlier in the chapter: "Why do you want more money?", evolved about 200,000 years ago. There, of course, they were exposed to very similar environmental conditions as elephants, giraffes or lions. Our human ancestors learned similar instincts and behavior patterns as the animals. And like us. For example, that an immediate reward through food, for example, is more important than anything else.

200,000 years ago, there were no banks or pensions or other things. No ancestor worried about his pension in 20 or 30 years because those stuff just didn't exist. Clearly, people have not sufficiently developed their sense of such important but only in the future things in their brains!

We are still almost no different from our ancient ancestors in terms of our brains and instincts. And this is now this creates difficulty for you, for me, for all people living in the 21st century. Today in Europe there is plenty of food, drink and shelter, so the immediate rewards are available everywhere. This could mean that all thoughts of our future could be quite unimportant in our daily lives and thoughts. But they

Saving - Start early and get rich faster!

absolutely are not, that's where we can be fooled. Because, as I said, this kind of reward is an innate instinct, so it's not something we have to learn. It stays with us whether we like it or not.

It's an "innate" weakness, so to speak. Something that was perfectly fine 200,000 years ago is still deeply ingrained in us. Even if we are already doing something completely different at the same time: We always and everywhere plan for the future. We plan the weekend on Monday, we plan our soccer training or the next riding lesson or try to save for a purchase in three years.

Our focus has completely changed. We can no longer think and act like an elephant, giraffe or lion. We want and need to constantly plan ahead. We can certainly do that already, although our brains have hardly evolved in this respect.

Now the problem has become clearer, hasn't it? This difficulty of planning for the future and focusing on it, keeping a goal in mind, persevering - that's something we don't always find easy in many areas of life.

If things were different, adults would have been, for example, much more determined about climate change for at least 30 years. It's long been known that the earth is warming, and sea levels are rising. But the consequences of that seemed so distant. If its immediacy were truly understood, so much would have to be done because people would have been downright frightened. Often enough, in current situations with future consequences, nothing is done. Adults often feel the same way when it comes to saving, making provisions for retirement and many other financial matters. One buys rather the new, mad shoes rather than saving that cash. And at some point, the hole in the till is so big that it's almost impossible to fix. It's a bit like climate change.

▶ What can you do now in concrete terms?

First of all, you should be aware that everyone has the weakness of preferring instant reward to saving and providing for the future.

Secondly, you can make a more conscious decision to save now.

Third, you should have a goal that you want to save for. To help you, you can answer the following questions and fill in your answers below ...

What do you dream of, what would you like to have?

1. (a Ferrari, a dog, ...)
2.
3.

Only with a clear goal in mind you have a real reason to save money now. This is called motivation. It's like going on vacation with your parents. If you don't have a goal, for example, "We're going to Holland by car and want to get there Saturday afternoon," but just drive off, you'll never

Saving - Start early and get rich faster!

arrive somewhere and be able to say, "This is exactly where we wanted to go, this is our vacation destination."

It is important to have your goals in mind. You should have thought about them yourself. Then they will definitely increase your motivation to save money. Because then you'll know exactly what you're saving for.

But you should also be careful not to make saving too difficult for yourself. For example, by trying to save everything - really everything. And not spending anything at all. That might work for a short time, but eventually you'll probably feel sad because you can't buy anything anymore. And then you'll start spending money on unnecessary items again. So, I recommend saving sustainably, not 100%, of your money!

On the other hand, the amount of money you save must have a certain amount, so that you also have a sum available with which you can become rich. More about this in the next chapters.

It is clear that it does not make sense to save 100%, but also not only five percent of your money. So, it's a good compromise to keep using half of your pocket money and cash gifts to buy nice things. That's still a big percentage. With that, you shouldn't get into a situation where you feel like you can't treat yourself to anything.

You should save a quarter (25%) in a bank account. You can use this money for concrete goals. Such goals can be things you want to buy in two or three or more months.

The remaining 25% should be saved for a much longer time.

It is best not to touch it at all. This money will make you rich! You should really, really never spend it again and not buy things with it, no matter how great the temptation. I call this "putting money away."

▶ What's my recommendation?

I recommend that you put away 25% of your allowance and money gifts (birthday, Christmas, and so on) for a specific savings goal, preferably one from the list on the previous page.

Another 25% you should save away and not spend at all. This is the foundation for getting rich and will be invested later!

How to get rich with this 25%, I will explain in the next chapter. You might need a little help from your parents.

And please do not forget: You still have half of your money left over! With it you can continue to buy toys, books and other things that every child likes and needs to grow up. I have summarized this pictorially once again for you:

Saving - Start early and get rich faster!

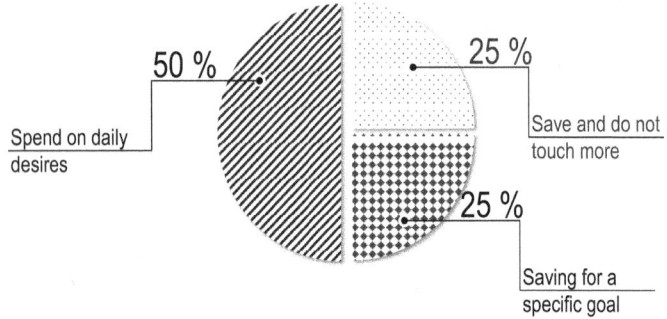

Of course, you will get rich faster if you don't spend so much money on toys, that's clear. Nevertheless, you should also have fun in life, and sometimes that includes treating yourself to something.

In order to check how much money you get approximately per year, we will calculate it for the past year.

Last year	single	Extrapolated for one year	product
Pocket money (per week)	€	x 52	€
or			
Pocket money (per month)	€	x 12	€
Birthday money	€	x 1	€
Christmas/Easter or other (religious) festivals	€	x 1	€
Other money	€	x 1	€
Other money	€	x 1	€
Sum (Attention: of course you can add the pocket money only once)			€

Saving - Start early and get rich faster!

At the beginning you distinguish whether you get your pocket money per week or per month. In the example we say you get 2 € per week. You enter this in the first line after "Pocket money (per week)".

Then you have to take the 2 € for the 52 weeks of a year with 52 times (this is the "product" in mathematics, so 2 € x 52). The result is 104 €. That's how much you get in a year. You enter this in the first row in the last column under "Product". You do the same with birthday money and so on. If you don't have an entry for any of the provided rows, for example in "Other money", then enter a zero there. At the end there should be something in each row.

After completing the chart, the last column under "Product" (plus calculate) can be summed and you'll have the result at the big €-sign. This is the total money you got last year. Not bad, right? If it's not enough, think together with your parents how you can manage to earn more money.

Tip: Since some months have five weeks instead of four, it's smart to get your pocket money per week instead of per month. Example: You get 10 € per month. Then you ask your parents if you can get 2,5 € per week (there are four weeks in a month). For months with five weeks you will get 12,5 €. Maybe you can persuade your parents □

What money can you save next?

1.

2.

Saving - Start early and get rich faster!

3. _____

What are your daily wishes? (You have half of your money available for this, which is the 50% share from the chart above).

1. _____
2. _____
3. _____

What are your specific savings goals? (25% share from the graph above)

1. _____
2. _____
3. _____

▶ What do you learn by saving?

- To plan for the future by thinking about what you would like to own or buy someday.
- To be conscientious with money.
- Saving for its own sake and a sense that you can get by with less money.

> This is very important; it limits the compulsive desire for "more".
>
> And by the way you will have taken your first steps to becoming rich.

The earlier you learn to save, the easier it will be. When you learned to speak as a child, you also started with single words. This was difficult enough for you and took some time, but it was part of the learning process. Your parents supported you and praised or corrected you, but you had to do it yourself. Today, speaking is totally normal for you, just like breathing. You don't have to think about it, you do it automatically. You will feel the same way if you start saving early. It may seem complicated or difficult at first, and you may make mistakes. But the more you get used to it and the more you get involved with money, saving that money and reaching your goals will become automatic for you. Again, definitely get your parents to help you with this.

Of course, you can learn how to speak (for example, a foreign language) as well as how to save money when you are older or even grown up. But as a child, you can simply get a head start. Everything is a little easier. Another advantage of starting early is that getting rich usually takes time. Therefore, it's even more important that you start as early as possible.

We will see in the next chapter that some so-called investments pay off even more if you are patient and wait for some time. It is not bad to have learned this as early as possible. But more about that in the next two chapters.

So, "Start early and get rich faster!"

By the way, investment refers to a (long-term) investment of money. The word actually comes from Latin and means "to clothe." Funny how original words are used quite differently today!

Investing - how you get more with less!

Isabel sat in her orchard, gazing lovingly at her four grandchildren playing tag among the old, bony trees. Helena came running to her, her long blonde hair fluttering in the wind. Out of breath, she asked, "Grandma, how old are these trees anyway?"

Isabel cleared her throat, "They're almost as old as I am ..."

"How old are you?" asked Helena, grinning curiously.

"I'm seventy-nine years old, sweetheart," Grandma replied.

Helena's eyes snapped open, "Whoa, that's old, well, the

trees I mean." She grinned again.

"Yes, I was about your age when my family planted the trees," Isabel said, looking dreamily across the large orchard.

"We had to help here every week to keep the garden thriving. I often had to pull weeds or water the young little trees when it was too dry. It was exhausting, but we also had a lot of fun doing it."

Helena's eyes widened again, and she now looked at the huge meadow herself.

"That doesn't look like fun to me ... that just looks like a lot of work!" she then said thoughtfully.

Isabel smiled gently, "It was, child. We didn't have a TV or a car back then, and all I had to play with were my siblings and our parents, of course. We played every free minute and the not free minutes we tried to play. Plucking weeds quickly turned into a competition to see which of us was faster. With that, the time flew by. Today you spend far too much time sitting alone in your rooms playing alone."

Helena replied, "I see," her expression didn't exactly underscore it, as she raised her eyebrows and looked more questioning than understanding.

After a moment's thought, she added, "Thank you Grandma, thanks to you, I can now eat such delicious apples, cherries and plums."

Helena bit into a crisp apple, put three more in the basket that was next to Grandma's feet and sprinted back to her siblings.

"Yes my dear, sometimes good things just take time, for that we and all future generations will have something from the garden for a long time" whispered Isabel softly. A tear of happiness silently rolled down her cheek.

▶ What have you learned?

- If you work hard for something and invest time, it's worth it. And most of the time, you eventually get something back (almost for free).
- Sometimes you work hard for a long time for something in the here and now without any visible result. But the future result is all the greater for it! An apple tree, for example, takes almost ten years to bear apples that can be harvested.
- Community helps not only in weeding, but also in investing and investing money, because you can share the work (the so-called invest or your search results).

- It's always wise to ask experienced people, like your grandparents or parents, for advice. This way you can avoid making the same mistakes that thousands of people have made before you.
- Good things sometimes take a little longer, sometimes generations as in the example of Helena and Isabel. A generation lasts about 30 years. Between Isabel and Helena there are even more than two generations, namely 70 years.

Helena's grandmother, together with her family, has "invested" a lot of time in the orchard. They have taken time and cared for the young trees. From this, they were able to make a profit in the form of a fruit harvest. You can do the same with money: Invest it, get a profit with a little time and patience, and become rich with it. I will explain how to do that in the next chapter.

These investments exist!

There are different ways of investing, that is, different ways of making more out of little money without having to work for it. I will now introduce you to some of the most important ones:

The bank

The best known way to invest your money and make less become more is the bank. The principle of a bank and how you profit from it is explained in this section:

Hannes has saved 100 €. He doesn't need this money at the moment, so he takes it to the bank on World Savings Day at the end of October and puts it in his savings account. The bank takes this money and "works" with it, lending it out or making its own investments. The bank does nothing else with Hannes' money than what you are trying to do with this book: namely, to earn money without doing any work of its own, i.e. without producing a product itself, for example.

The bank lends money on and gets interest for it (explanation on the next page.) Or the bank buys valuable products, which it sells again later for even more money. Again, more on this in the next chapter.

It is important to understand that the bank can do whatever it wants with your money - or with Hannes' money. In doing so, it always tries to achieve making the sum into more. That's why you can learn a lot from the banks and their strategies.

As a reward/fee Hannes gets 2 € after one year, because he lent his money to the bank. Thus 100 € have become 10**2** € after one year, without Hannes having to work for it.

Some terms as explanation and summary

Hannes has thus:

> invested 100 €
>
> got 2 € interest
>
> got 2% interest
>
> 2 € profit made

This is shown in the chart on the next page above.

These investments exist!

Investing or "investing" money means that someone gives his money to the bank. The bank works with it, lends it on, for example, and after a year gets **more** money back as a thank you. The "more money" is also called interest

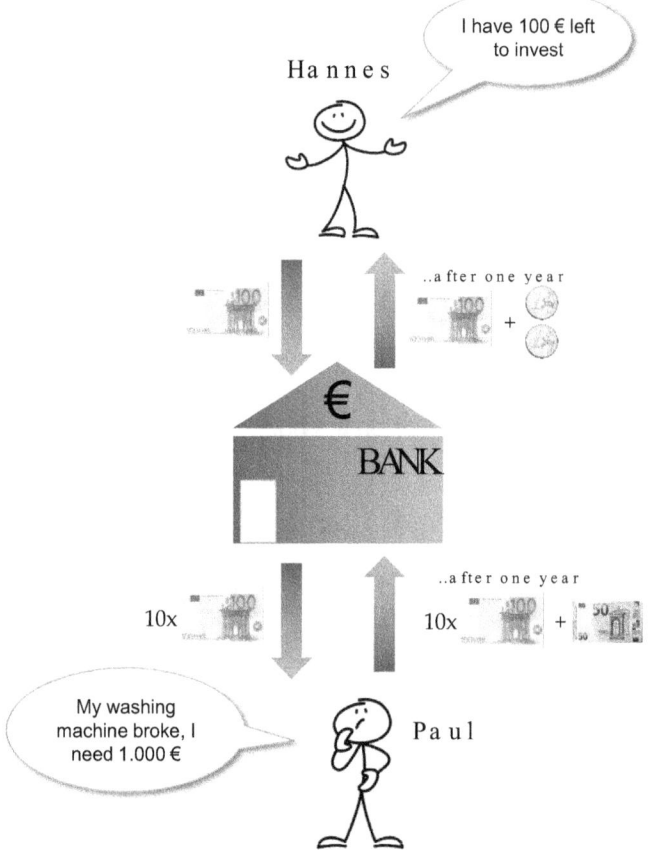

"**Borrowing**" means someone does not have enough money himself and asks the bank to give him a sum (lend). After, for example, one year you have to pay back the money + a fee for borrowing

These investments exist!

Paul's washing machine is broken and he urgently needs a new one. It will cost him €1,000. But since Paul has not saved the money, he asks the bank for a loan. A loan means that the bank lends Paul the money. The bank lends Paul 1,000 € and charges him a fee of €50 after one year. This gives Paul time to save the €1,000 €and pay the bank back including the 50 € interest. You can see this in the chart at the bottom.

So, Paul has:

    received €1000 credit/borrowed money

    paid €50 interest

You can see that in the previous chart below.

Interest is a kind of consideration or fee that you must pay when you are lent money. In our example we use the word interest both when someone gets money (for example Hannes gets 2 € interest, the bank pays him the fee because Hannes lent the money to the bank) or also pays money (for example Paul pays 50 € fee because he had to borrow the money).

The concept of the bank is very simple: so long as enough people give their money to the bank, the bank always has a lot of money available. Although it does not own the money, the bank is allowed to use it and work with it, invest it or even lend it to others. In our example from above, the bank needs €1,000 to be able to lend this money on. So, for example, it takes €100 from ten people (10 x €100 = €1,000). This

These investments exist!

means that the bank has to pay all ten people €2 after one year. The bank has to pay a total of 20 €.

On the other hand, it gets 50 € from Paul as loan fee/interest after one year. If we then look at the balance sheet, we see:

After one year

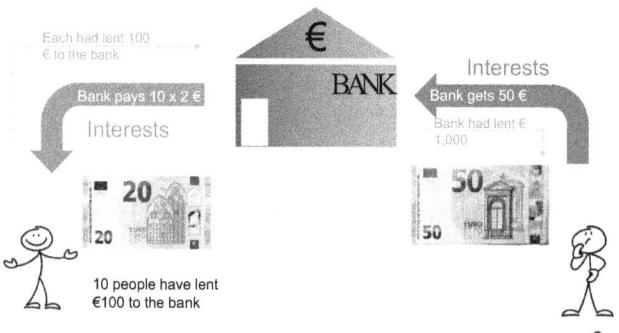

The bank makes a profit of 30 € in this example.

This is a very simple example. Banks also lend money to large companies like Volkswagen or entire countries. We are then immediately talking about money in the billions. That is a number with nine zeros.

So, the European Bank lent all of Europe €500,000,000,000 in 2021 because of the Corona pandemic. That's a lot of money.

Just as a reminder, here are the orders of magnitude of the

These investments exist!

numbers:

Thousand 1.000

million 1.000.000

Billions 1.000.000

Trillions 1.000.000.000

And so on. Germany, for example, has 1.9 trillion €in debt to the banks ... one can hardly imagine. Of course, the concept is only worthwhile for the banks if they get more money than they must pay to Hannes, for example. But that doesn't always work either. A bank can also "go bust" if it has miscalculated on large investments.

These investments exist!

Conclusion♪

Borrowing money is sometimes necessary, as with Paul in our example. Adults also borrow money when they need very large amounts of money because they want to, for example, build a house. Most of the time, however, borrowing money and paying interest is not good, especially for smaller amounts of money for things you don't really need, like the newest TV when the old one still works. Those who borrow money often pay interest spread over several months, which then add up to a lot of money and prevent you from actually saving for the whole year! Therefore, better save the money for such a purchase.

Side note: It concerns with the explanation the fundamental principle of a bank. High interest rates are not obtained unfortunately up-to-date any longer, which has however clearly more complex reasons, which are not explained in this book. As the book goes to press in October 2022, interest rates on savings deposits are rising slightly again.

These investments exist!

The principle of supply and demand

This section is about investing in products.

You may have heard of the saying, "supply and demand determine price." I would like to explain this to you with an example that you could apply yourself right away. Talk to your parents about this saying as they will likely have great examples of this concept drawn from their own experience.

LEGO TECHNIC® has produced some products, for example a large excavator, for only three years. Many products even much shorter time. You get one of these excavators for Christmas and you are happy. The excavator has cost your parents 100 €.

One year after the end of production of the excavator, one of your friends discovers your great toy and wants to have the same excavator. But you don't give yours away and say to him: "Why don't you buy one yourself? Your friend's father looks up LEGO TECHNIK ® on the Internet and sees that this excavator is no longer sold.

So the demand for this product in our example is 1 (your friend) and the supply from Lego is 0 (there are none left). When this is the case, high prices are usually the result. This is because the demand is greater than the supply.

These investments exist!

Rule of thumb♠

As a rule of thumb, you can remember: few or rare products with high demand (that is, something that many people want) means high prices.

So, since your friend can't officially buy the LEGO toy anymore, they make you an offer. The conversation might go like this:

Friend (F): "I'll offer you 70 € for your excavator, it's not new anymore!"

You (Y): "But I would like to have 150 € for it, after all, you can no longer buy it officially. That makes it a collector's item."

F: "That's way too expensive!"

Y: "Then you can buy it somewhere else ☐"

F: "I don't know where, it's not available for purchase on the internet anymore."

Y: "I know, that's why I'll meet you halfway and give it to you for €140."

F: "I'll pay you 120 €!"

Y: "Ok, let's choose the golden mean: 130 €."

F: „Deal!"

So, you would have made a profit of 30 €. That is actually a rather realistic possible price increase a year after LEGO stopped production. Of course, the price depends a lot on which LEGO set it is. Rare or special editions are even more expensive, others cheaper. By the way, the best price is achieved when the LEGO toy is still in its original packaging.

The "market", i.e. the trade in goods, works in a similar way for other products such as wine, houses, stamps, cars and many other things that people need or collect. It applies the other way around as well. If the supply is high, or the demand is low, the price will be low, and no strong price increase would be expected. Take a toothpick as an example.

Practice:

Think with your parents about what products or things you know of that could see an increase in value.

1.

2.

3.

These investments exist!

The stock market

The stock market, such as the "Frankfurt Stock Exchange", which is the best-known stock exchange in Germany, also functions according to exactly the aforementioned principle of supply and demand. You can imagine the stock market as a huge marketplace where you can buy and sell (almost) anything. But the whole thing is traded worldwide and nowadays almost exclusively online, i.e. via computer or cell phone.

If you own a share, it means you own a part of a company. To build an example, let's say you have shares of Apple. Shares in major companies are usually very, very small, but you still have the right to vote on the future of the company. This can be done, for example, at the general meeting, where important decisions about the future are voted on. Here, not only the head of the company may then decide, but he must also consult the share owners. Apple currently has (as of May 2020) issued 4.3 billion shares, i.e. "sold". From this you can see: With one share, you still don't have too much of a say in the company. Nevertheless, you play an important role as a so-called shareholder. This simply means: You are someone who owns a share.

This worldwide marketplace also means: You can sell your share, i.e. your value in the company, to a woman from Japan without ever having met or even knowing each other. You can set the price for your share as you wish, with the risk that no one will buy your share. Again, supply and demand determine how much you really get for your product, the stock in this case.

These investments exist!

The difficulty is to precisely estimate „supply and demand" because worldwide influences determine both. You can own a share that was valued at 50 € but due to a war in a distant country, the demand for your share drops very strongly and suddenly it is only worth 5 €.

Why is this example realistic? A war is a very, very bad situation in which people are afraid for their survival. In such a time, the desire to buy a certain product will tend to decrease. It is possible that the product could even disappear from the market altogether. People would have to focus on completely different things: protection or escape, for example. Demand for some products will then drop to zero, just like demand for stocks, because people won't spend money on them in an emergency. As demand drops to zero, the price responds accordingly and drops as well.

As a reminder, supply and demand determine the price. You can see this, for example, on the Frankfurt Stock Exchange: The so-called share price shows you the current value of (d)a share.

A war situation is an extreme situation, which I use as an example to explain the influences on the stock market. There are many other, much less visible influences. The influences impair people's desire to buy. Of course, it's not just a war that determines the price of the stock. There are many other influences.

Fortunately, the opposite can also happen. For example: the company you co-"own" could develop a great new product that everyone wants. Maybe a new shampoo that smells especially good. Everyone wants it and therefore, demand for the product increases. And with that increased shampoo

These investments exist!

demand, the demand for the company that produces this shampoo also escalates. As a result of the rising demand, the value of the share in the company rises. If you sold your stock at that time, you could make a profit.

Figure: DAX progression in points over years, significant increase visible in ten years.

The picture above shows the course of the German Share Index (DAX), which summarizes the 30 largest companies on the stock exchange. (Since September 2021, 40 companies are shown in the DAX, i.e. "listed"). The DAX is thus intended to show the performance of the entire German stock market and can be seen as a kind of average of the German economy.

What do you see there?

You see on the left, y-axis at the time of 2012 (on the horizontal x-axis) about 7,000 points, up to about 14,000 points in 2022 a big increase of about 7,000 points. Ifyou had

These investments exist!

invested an amount of €1,000 in the DAX in 2012, you would already have about €2,000 in 2022. Not bad, is it? You'll get that money in your bank account when you resell the shares. Of course, there are also some strong downward swings in the share performance above. These are crises or economic difficulties. (We will cover the topic of taxes in Volume II).

What happens if you just keep, or hold onto the stock? As a reward for putting your faith in a company and buying a stock, the company rewards you once a year and gives you money. This reward is called a dividend, and you can think of it as being like the interest you've already learned about at the bank. Because the advantage of the share for the company is that you give it money and get a part of the company in return. The company can use this money for their business activities such as developing new products or building new factories. Unlike the bank, however, this money belongs to the company, and the company doesn't have to give it back to you because you have made a trade: money for stock.

According to "Börse Online," there are about 50,000 companies listed on the stock exchange. To that, the countless commodities and all the other goods that can also be traded on the stock exchange must be added. In sum, the selection of stocks is very large. Since that was now a lot of new information at once, I would like to make a short summary: the DAX represents the German stock market. It can be seen as an average to check whether the economy is doing well or performing badly. In addition, you can see from the example from the last ten years of the DAX' that the price keeps rising. However, there are also critical times when the share price drops abruptly. Nevertheless, the DAX

These investments exist!

will continue to rise in the future. There are several reasons for this assumption: Firstly, the companies listed on the DAX will develop ever better products or offer new, necessary services. They can then sell these more expensively. All of this will increase the value of the company and thus the demand for that company's shares. This in turn increases the share price (keyword: supply and demand). Secondly, people always want more money (I explained this to you in the chapter "Why do people want more money?"), so there are always more people in the world investing in shares. That, too, increases demand, and you now know what that means.

Perhaps you've heard of inflation? It means that more and more money is being printed and therefore more money is in circulation. This usually causes product prices to rise. Since inflation usually keeps increasing, it causes prices to go up in the long run. Because shares are strongly linked to the products of companies and are therefore also a kind of "price", the value of shares also increases due to inflation. I will explain more about this in my second book. Ray Dalio has created a very good video on YouTube about this topic: "How the economic machine works".

I intentionally focused heavily on the DAX as an example because I can use it to explain the relationships relatively easily. However, the basic statements also apply to individual stocks (the DAX comprises 40 stocks or companies). In addition, I use the DAX again in the part your parents read.

These investments exist!

What do you learn from it?

1. Supply and demand determine the price, also on the stock exchange.
2. Try to always classify where you stand (price high or low?) before you buy something.
    a. It can be done by simply thinking.
    b. Thethe stock market and stock trends can be analyzed.
    c. There are various ratios and websites for a classification of the prices. I recommend the book by Susanne Levermann "The relaxed way to wealth". I would recommend reading this book together with an adult to help you understand the technical terms.
3. The stock market is very complex.
4. You can win a lot of money in the stock market, but you can also lose it. If it were otherwise, everyone would be rich.
5. All stock investors try to buy at a cheap price and sell at a more expensive price, yet it's not always clear what cheap means.
6. Companies, you can invest in, can also go bankrupt. This means that you, as an investor, lose a large part of your money. This is what distinguishes a share from a product, such as your LEGO excavator. Because you still own it, regardless of whether LEGO goes bankrupt or not.

This is how I get rich, Dad!

My steps to wealth

Now, I've given you some concrete suggestions in this book on how to get rich. Starting with simply saving by setting aside 25% of your money to create your first wealth, which can then grow all by itself through investing.

The most important thing here is patience, as compound interest will help you with most investments. (I'll explain what "interest rate" means in a moment.) Don't be discouraged by potential setbacks. Understanding the stock market simply takes time and experience. And very few people would claim to have understood everything about investing. You don't have to!

With the foundation you've built in this book and the helpful exercises in between, you'll have all the knowledge you need to get started on your own. Always get advice and help from your parents, friends or acquaintances who have already gained a lot of experience with money, savings and shares and are therefore "rich". Why not ask a rich friend of your parents, "Please explain to me how you got rich." He/she will be puzzled by the question, and you may be puzzled by the answer and learn something. Take heart in whatever you do, and you'll be rich!

I would like to give you now at the end 13 concrete steps, with which you become rich.

My steps to wealth

13 concrete steps what you can do now to become rich:

1. You need money that you can invest: Make a savings plan together with your parents.
    a. As a reminder, use 50% to play and have fun and save the other 50%. Here's my recommendation: save 25% on something you want to buy and use the remaining 25% to invest.
2. If you don't have enough money or you want to get rich even faster: Think about how you can earn more money. Maybe you can help your neighbors, you will surely think of something (this also applies to adults, they can for example look for a small side job if the actual earnings are not enough to invest).
3. Find out about products you want to invest in. LEGO is just one example. Note here: The more a product interests you personally, the easier it will be to trade it. If LEGO doesn't interest you, think about what else is out there. Rare comics, old Barbie dolls or something completely different ...
4. Only invest money that you don't need. If you lose it, it's bad, but it won't cause you financial hardship.
5. Look at every gain, but also every loss, as a lesson of life. Don't be sad, but do better next time. You will learn even more from the defeats than from the easy victories, because the defeats hurt you.
6. Read a lot of books. Why? Because reading educates and in a very short time you can experience and eventually learn the knowledge of decades of successful and exciting personalities. Besides, reading stimulates your brain to think (along). And is therefore very valuable. Especially if

My steps to wealth

you want to become rich. Thereby you can read all kinds of books ...
  a. Books about money/investments
  b. Novels - nothing better than exercising your imagination, even when it comes to investing.
  c. Non-fiction books about whatever interests you (horses, the environment, ships...) This will allow you to deepen your knowledge in a specialized field and who knows, maybe it will be of some use to you when investing. Most of all, it should be fun for you.
  d. Books about rich, famous, interesting people, biographies. It's a very easy way to broaden your horizons and get opinions and ideas about things you might not have even thought about before.
  Many successful people will tell you, "You are the sum of the books you read."

7. Learn from your friends and your parents how to get rich or how not to get rich. Negative examples are important, too.
8. Talk to your parents about money and finances and have them explain anything you don't understand.
9. Discuss with your parents whether you can open a savings account at a bank into which you can deposit money every month.
10. For the brave, consider with your parents whether you also want to set up an account for investing. I recommend simple "trader accounts" here, such as at Consorsbank. The fees are very low. I describe everything else about this especially for your parents in their part of this book.

11. Ask yourself the right questions such as: What do I have to do to become rich? You will see, your brain will magically suggest answers.
12. Never think: I can't afford that! That blocks you in your goal to become rich. The question should be: How can I afford this?
13. Don't let others tell you what is possible and what is not. And above all, evaluate whether that person is an expert in that particular field, or just has an opinion on the subject. You wouldn't ask Lionel Messi how a rocket works or a bank employee how to shoot the best free kick. Check whether someone is really helping you with their views or just trying to discourage you.

Think about further steps

_____'s own ideas for getting rich!

1.
2.
3.
4.
5.
6.

The magic for my wealth

Getting rich is actually very easy. I hope I've been able to show you that clearly so far. Why it is genuinely as easy as I say, has a simple mathematical reason, namely the so-called interest-interest.

The "principle of interests " means: you immediately reinvest the first interest you get back. So, the money you get for "doing nothing", or rather for your patience, is immediately reinvested. And on top, further interests are gained. By these interests, money increases. The principle is shown in the picture. On the left is the respective investment. On the right the interest including the investment. The investments are reflected by the visably smaller euro signs. From top to bottom goes the time axis, for example the first line is year 1, the second line is year 2 and so on. The bottom line is a much later point in time, here the money has already tripled! Unimaginable? No! Over a sufficiently large period of time, this is actually easily doable.

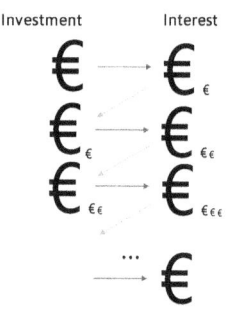

Your euros keep growing and growing. If you believe this very simple "miracle" and actively and patiently follow the most important advice, your saved money will grow incredibly fast. How fast, I will show you with the help of the next graphic:

The magic for my wealth

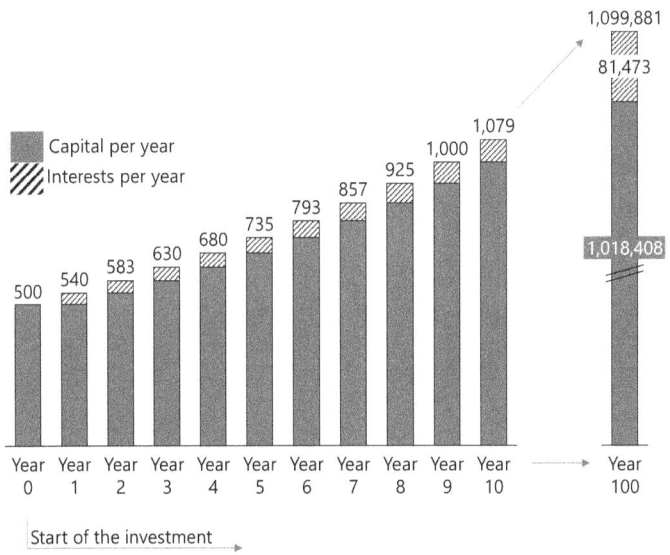

The graph shows the same principle of growing money as seen on the previous page, only with real numbers. In year 0, which could be this year for you, for example, 500 € are invested. And we assume a constant interest rate of 8%. Such an interest rate is not unrealistic on the stock market. However, it should serve here mainly as an example. The 500 € are shown as a bar in anthracite (far left). After one year (this is visible at the bottom of the horizontal axis) we have received the first 8% on our 500 €.

The calculation looks like this: $500 \text{ €} \times 8\% = 500 \text{ €} \times = 500 \text{ €} \times 0{,}08 = 40 \text{ €}$

The magic for my wealth

The 40 € are immediately reinvested, so that we do not get 40 € in the next year, but 43 € interest. In this way, we manage to have over €1,000 after ten years and over €1 million after 100 years. That is of course a very long time. It's just to show you how much money you can make "out of nothing".

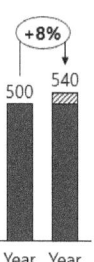

Out of curiosity, I calculated what you or I would have in money if our great-great-great-ancestor 200 years ago had invested €1,000 (or the same amount in the currency of the time) at 8% per year as well. Hold on - we would have €4,838,949,585 ... that's almost €5 billion. That would put us in 35th place among the richest Germans, according to Wikipedia[1]. Crazy!

It is once again illustrated how the power of the compound effect works. I don't know about you, but to me it seems like a missed opportunity by our ancestors that they didn't bequeath us this incredibly large sum. We, in turn, have the chance to do better for ourselves, our children and grandchildren and great-grandchildren. Please note: All of the calculation examples presented here are presented without the cost of buying shares, without taxes, and without the impact of inflation. I will address these issues in my next book.

---

[1] https://de.wikipedia.org/wiki/Liste_der_500_reichsten_Deutschen

Timetable of getting rich

In this chapter, I will present a very specific timetable to you: What steps should you take on the path of getting rich?

I'm sure you can read this book in a few days. You might need a little longer to internalize it. Or you may read it more than once (for support, feel free to regularly check the last chapter in the book "Summary"). As a reading period I would assume that it would take about three months.

Take your time when reading the book! Write down the topics from the book that are important or interesting to you, just for yourself. Keeping this information as a kind of diary is a good way to do this. I have created a suggestion at the end of the book that you can use immediately. There you can, for example, briefly summarize books that have shaped, influenced and encouraged you.

The advantage of a diary is that you can quickly, within a few minutes, refresh the knowledge gained of entire books. Over time, your diary will grow and you will be able to expand your knowledge. You can also record your own ideas and thoughts in this "diary": What things do you want to invest in? What have you learned or experienced? Writing those things down helps you a lot to learn from your own mistakes and to repeat successful things.

Timetable of getting rich

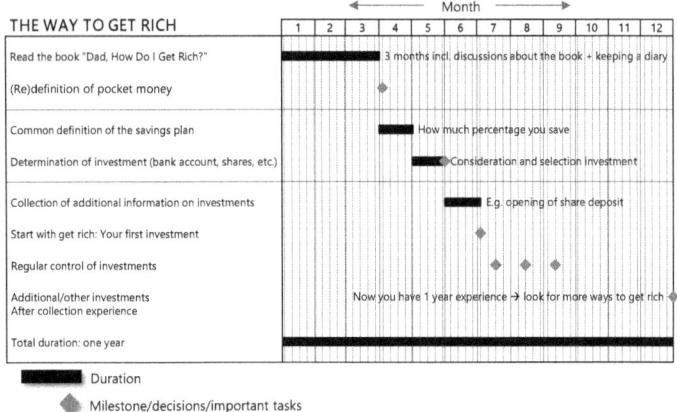

After you have read the book, decide with your parents on the amount of your pocket money, or adjust it as described above.

Then you will be able to define a savings plan together with your parents. Suggestions about percentages of savings are in the chapter "Saving - start early and get rich faster!". I suggest you a time frame of two weeks for this important task. Again, you will certainly accomplish the actual defining faster than in two weeks. There is the saying "one should sleep on important decisions overnight". Two extra weeks give you the opportunity to think about your ideas and to discuss advantages and disadvantages. And with "you" I mean you and your parents.

The next step, "Determining investments", is the most important and, together with the next task, "Gathering additional information on investments", takes a total of three months. At these two points, you determine what you want to invest in and then gather additional information so that you have a good knowledge base before you get started. At the same time, please note that it is difficult to be able to gather all the information fully on one topic.

The lack of "all available information" shouldn't stop you from taking your first steps towards getting rich! It is better to invest 100 € with some risk in an investment than to do nothing at all. What can happen? In the worst case you lose the money and learn a lot for the future. And in the best case, the investment pays off and you make a great deal! Besides, you should only invest money that you could do without in the worst case. Of course, 100 € as a child is a lot of money, but a little courage is necessary so that you can become rich. So dare to do it!

At first glance, the time frame for these two tasks looks like a very long time at three months. Again, good things often take a little longer to come to a good decision. Since you will certainly want to discuss some of the information with your parents, and you certainly can't talk about it every day, the process may even drag on a little longer. If you can come to a good decision sooner, all the better. Please don't lose patience. This step will probably seem long. Since investments are long-term investments, those three months don't matter. Think of it as a good exercise in patience.

Your first investment can be anything (LEGO, savings book, stock ...). I recommend opening a bank account right away with money flowing into it on a regular basis. I put this important milestone at the end of the previous three months. Regularly can also mean once a year, say always after Christmas. I also recommend investing in stocks, or more

Timetable of getting rich

precisely in ETFs[2].. Savings plans are available for as little as €25 per month. That should definitely be left after what you learned in my book. With this you would already save 300 € per year and profit from a long-term development of the market.

Regardless of this timeline, have regular, "official" conversations with your parents about money and finances. Educate yourselves together and thus set further "milestones" in becoming rich. The educational progress can be done very easily via books, YouTube videos or the like on topics such as real estate, stocks, etc.

One piece of advice from me about this timeline, as I myself am also a very impatient person and would prefer to have all the results immediately: people overestimate what you can achieve in a year. And they underestimate what you can achieve in ten years. Please don't underestimate your progress in the long run. Remember where you were ten years ago? I bet you have already achieved a lot in that time. For example, if you're 13 years old now, you've gone from a three-year-old to a teenager, passing through developmental milestones along the way. What all have you learned in those ten years? That's a much more visible and measurable difference than the difference between a 13-year-old and a 14-year-old.

---

[2] ETFs are a special form of shares, an explanation I give in the part for your parents further back. It's best to talk to your parents about what ETFs are exactly. The important thing for you is: they help you to get rich. ☺

Now you can say that dramatic changes always happen with children within ten years. Isn't that also the case when you compare a thirteen-year-old with a 23-year-old? Or you ask your parents what they have learned and experienced in ten years. If you think about it, you will probably agree with me that in ten years you have often become a "different person". You will experience these big differences in just ten years with persistence and perseverance, will and fun also in the field of finances! If you do it right, you will become a rich person.

.

On the way to wealth, you must not forget ...

On the way to wealth, you must not forget ...

Of course, this book is about money and how you can make it become more money. Also, you understood why money is important. However, for me it is equally important to clarify that money is first and foremost a means to an end. And you should look at it the same way. Money opens opportunities for you in life to do or buy things that **would be more difficult without money.**

However, if you are sad or lonely, or have few goals, no amount of money will make you happy! You always have many opportunities to do great things with and without money. Therefore, money is not important. This sounds like a contradiction in terms, so let me explain briefly:

Love, happiness, contentment and especially health are the really important things in life that money can't buy. You must not forget that on your way to wealth. At the same time, these values must not be used as an excuse, along the lines of "Why should I get rich, health is much more important ..." Why not work on both?

I'm sure you'll agree that if all these basic requirements are met in terms of love, health and so on, it's cooler to have more money and therefore more opportunities than less. That's what my book is about. Don't let general sayings like "money doesn't make you happy" dissuade you from your goal of becoming rich. In my opinion, these are often just excuses to not even try.

Final word for you

One's whole life is a learning process. I hope you see it that way too. And, I hope you use this book as a building block in your learning process. It will take time, but it will be worth it for you. I hope you enjoy investing and getting rich. Above all, see the process of learning and getting rich as a constant challenge in which you should have a maximum of fun. I am sure that you will also develop a fascination for the possibilities what to do with "money". Because money is nothing else. It offers you possibilities. What you want to do with it is as diverse and unique as your personality. Therefore, consider getting rich as a chance to realize goals, even if you simply give the money away in the end.

Don't let it get you down and always remember: There has never been an investor who hasn't lost money at some point. I'm looking forward to meeting you in person, write me your story and successes or contact me by mail if you have any questions: goergantisch@gmail.com.

Many greetings

Your

Michael Goergen

From here begins part II of the book:

"For all parents of rich children"

Introduction for parents: How to use this book effectively

Since this is not a novel or a classic children's book, I ask you to observe how strongly your child is motivated to read the book by themselves. Of course, the ideal case is that they read through the book independently. However, if they are not so motivated, here are some ideas of what you can do to help it read:

1. If your child is not self-motivated to read the book, read the book aloud and tell matching stories from your own life. Your child will likely find it exciting to hear examples from mom or dad from their youth.
2. Don't force the book on your child, use quiet, relaxed moments (perhaps the summer vacation together) to introduce the book to your child.
3. You know your child best and know what and how to motivate him or her most effectively. Here, people like to distinguish between two basic types: People who are motivated "toward something," such as getting rich. Then there is the type of person who is motivated "away from something," that is, by an avoidance. For example, by avoiding being "poor." While this sounds similar, it is completely different for the motivational approach. Both for you and for your child. What is it like for your child? Pay attention and, if you're not sure, test different approaches to motivation.
4. Create an incentive for reading and working through the book, such as visiting the zoo, going to the movies, or going swimming together. Be a good motivator.

5. Take notes while reading and encourage your child to do the same. No one has ever gotten rich from reading alone, but only from the actions that follow. And this implementation is easier for you and your child if you can write down ideas, concepts or concrete actions in your own words and then take them to hand again and again. You will see that this is more efficient, and above all more effective, than looking up certain things again and again in a book. It is always your own words and thoughts that are best remembered. Besides, what you have noted down once sticks better in your memory. I therefore recommend keeping an excellence diary. More on this later in the text and in the last chapter.
6. I have included simple exercises and reflections. Feel free to do these together with your child and also, think about what you would write about. Then you can compare. Your child will probably find it quite exciting to see what mom or dad's goals, dreams, or wishes are.
    a. At the end of the book, you will find a schedule for one year with concrete suggestions for you and your child to implement. It is best to work through this after you have read the book.
7. Surely your child will also be motivated by the prospect of investing 100€ together with you at the end.

Basically, this book is nothing but one of the most important homework assignments your child will do. As a father of two, academic achievement and all subjects of learning are hugely important to me. However, for "real life", binomial formulas or the exact date when the French Revolution took place or how van Gogh executed his brush strokes are often not that crucial. Therefore, it is important to me to expand the broad knowledge based gained through formal schooling through this book on finance and thus offer a parallel subject of education for real life.

For all parents of rich children

While your child is reading the "rich kids" part, in this section of the book I have gathered what you can do as support and motivation for your child. The subject area of "investing" is completely new to your child and, unfortunately, not something he or she would have heard of or learned in school. Therefore, it is very important that you help your child understand this topic. Just as you would perhaps support them with a new school subject in the beginning. You are therefore a parent, teacher and above all, a role model all rolled into one person focusing on "finances".

If you are already well versed in investing and perhaps own stocks, real estate or the like yourself, you will find part of this section of the book a refresher. If investing is also rather new to you, feel free to also read through your child's part from the beginning, there you will find some ideas and background information around finance.

I've also summarized how you can help your child understand the topics of money, finance, and investing using specific examples. Just like your child learned to walk and talk back then, this topic also needs to be learned. The earlier your child starts, the better he or she will understand finances later. It is also important to "fall down" sometimes. Just as with any other subject matter your child has learned, he or she must have his or her own experiences with money topics. Or did you learn to walk or talk FOR the child? Of course not! You observed, lovingly supported and praised walking and talking when they made progress.

In addition to additional explanations about interest and

interest-interest that you can pass on to your child, I also have savings recommendations for you as an adult. If you already have your own savings plans/trader accounts or similar set up and working well, feel free to skip this chapter or match your approach with my suggestions.

I conclude the "Parents of Rich Kids" chapter with some general ideas and tips that are also independent of money, and also show a timeline in the kids section on how to proceed in getting rich with your child and which steps make sense and when.

What can you do for your rich child!

No matter how rich or poor you are or feel: Please pay your child some **pocket money**. It doesn't have to be a lot; especially for young children under the age of nine, I recommend only a few euros a month.

One of the main reasons why successful business founders cannot pass on their business to an equally successful heir (daughter or son) is the lack of education in financial topics of the offspring. There will be many reasons for this: too little time because the business is always in the foreground, disinterest on the part of the child, etc. The sparse time due to working for the company must be balanced with enthusiasm for financial topics to still introduce the children to entrepreneurship and finance. Even if you don't run your own business, share your experiences, positive or negative, early on. That's where pocket money is a very simple tool you can use to start early. It is a good way for your child to learn how to handle money and how to realize that "money just doesn't grow on trees." In this learning process, it also helps immensely if your child does not get everything from you, but either has to buy things himself or is told clearly that something cannot be bought (at the moment). And your child will only learn how to handle money if they manage (small amounts of) money.

How is a child supposed to find motivation or feel motivated if they constantly recieve the message that everything will fly to you and your family anyway? This feeling is also conveyed to children when you yourself are perhaps not rich but want to buy your child everything for precisely this reason, "because he or she should one day be better off than you were back then." Or if money is never discussed in the family as a matter of principle.

▶ Why pocket money?

- It is a first contact with money, with it one learns: What is a lot, what is little money? Your child recognizes this when he or she sees how much one can or cannot afford with 5 € per month.
- It can create the motivation to earn more on their own.
- This can lead to children being proud of being able to afford something themselves.

The Youth Welfare Office recommends specific amounts of pocket money depending on age. The amount is summarized in the table below. From the age of six, however, I recommend reducing the sums slightly and making them variable instead. Your child can reach the full amount by doing smaller but regular chores. This can be anything from regularly taking out the trash to cleaning, emptying the dishwasher. I recommend paying the money in full but making clear agreements with your child about the tasks. Don't overburden your child and please only cancel the pocket money in extreme emergencies. Your child should also be able to rely on you.

With increasing age, the variable part of the pocket money can increase and with age, of course also the tasks. Please note that your child should not have the choice of not doing a task and then settling for less money. This is the wrong incentive. Motivate them to energetically do their share in the family.

Age of the child	Recommended pocket money (Youth Welfare Office)	My recommendation (Variable part in %)	My recommendation (without variable part in €, rounded)
4-5 years	0.5 € / week	- 0 %	0.5 € / week
6-7 years	1.5 – 2 € / week	- 10…20 %	1.2 – 1.8 € / week
8-9 years	2 – 3 € / week	- 10…20 %	1.6 – 2.7 € / week
10-11 years	13 – 16 € / month	- 20 %	10 – 13 € / month
12-13 years	18 – 22 € / month	- 20 %	14 – 18 € / month
14-15 years	25 – 30 € / month	- 20 %	20 – 24 € / month
16-17 years	35 – 45 € / month	- 30 %	25 – 30 € / month
18 years	70 € / month		Dependent on own job[1]

[1] 30 € basic pocket money; pay more pocket money only if own money is also earned (maximum: 50 €)

Bear in mind, that it is a very, very big boost for your child's personal development, the so-called soft skills, if they work. The type of job doesn't matter. Be it in a restaurant as a waiter, where your child learns professional contact with people, in a supermarket stocking shelves, mowing the lawn or anything else. Discipline and a sense of responsibility are always necessary, and both are very important character traits.

What can you do for your rich child!

In the conclusion of the section for children, I recommend, among other things, a Trader account and your own bank account. I recommend you set up both accounts. Why? Because this way your child can learn the most about money, banking, saving and stock markets. By doing this, you give him/her a chance to manage money on his/her own, and at the same time, the Trader account provides a very simple way for you to "grow" the money together. The trader account will be the cornerstone by which your child will have internalized the topic of saving and investing by the time he/she is 16, so that by then your child can almost stand on his/her own two feet and manage his/her finances more independently. Again, in detail:

▶ Reasons for a savings account

- Learning how to handle savings/money
- Getting to know banks
- Realizing how time and saving can work wonders.
- Taking responsibility
- Learning independence in dealing with money
- Setting savings goals (together with you)

And just as important...

▶ Reasons for a Trader account

- First contact with shares/ETF
- Thereby understanding the stock market
- Learning to deal with and endure loss in the stock market as well.
- Achieve first profits!

If you yourself know a lot about stocks and have been able to celebrate successes, buy for your child one of your favorite stocks or stocks of something your child is enthusiastic about (PCs, cell phones, cars, toys ...). Watch the progress regularly, maybe once a month when there is pocket money. I don't recommend checking on the stocks/ETFs every day, your child should learn that patience also matters if you want to get rich in the long run. Critically discuss the stock's performance: has it gone up or down? What were the possible reasons?

If, however, you have no experience yourself or have had little experience with the stock market, I recommend the so-called ETFs - Exchange Traded Funds. An ETF is not an investment in one stock alone, but in a stock index, such as the German Dax, for example. The huge advantage of this is that the fees are virtually zero, unlike with equity funds. This saves you several percentage points, especially in the long term! This can make a difference of several hundred euros over ten years (see also next chapter), depending of course on how much money you have invested. In addition, you spread the risk over 40 stocks (in the Dax example) and are not dependent on a single sector. More about this in the next chapter as well.

Talk to your child in general about money and goals (for example, when buying a car), but not about financial hardships (that stresses them too much!). Relationships are especially important for the child's understanding: How long does it take to pay off a house on a certain salary? Things like that.

In general:

Read books to your child, gladly this one, but also anything else you can think of. To stay with the theme of "getting rich," you could also pick up books that deal with the theme of money, wealth, gold and treasure in novel form, such as Treasure Island, The Count of Monte Cristo, Aladdin, Alibaba and the 40 Thieves.... This will bring your child into contact with these themes in an even more playful way.

Motivate your child appropriately to read this book here, for example, by letting your child read the book for 30 minutes and arranging a "reward" beforehand, such as a visit to the cinema when the book is read through, eating ice cream or a small amount of money per number of pages. Afterwards, your child can, for example, tell you in detail about what he or she has read or even summarize a few paragraphs in writing about the content, much like a German homework assignment.

The power of the compound effect

Robert Kiyosaki, the author of one of my favorite books, "Rich dad, poor dad," included a great story in his book. Mr. Kiyosaki speaks "of one of the wonders of our time," the power of the compound effect. The purchase of Manhattan Island, on which the city of New York is built, is considered one of the greatest bargains in human history. The Dutch purchased the island from the Indians living there in 1626 for 60 guilders (old Dutch currency before the introduction of the Euro). This is about 30 €. Sounds little for such a valuable island today? Yes, certainly.

Only: If the Dutch had invested these 30 € at 8% interest per year on the stock exchange, they would have 440 trillion (!) € today, i.e. a 4 with 14 zeros. With that, they could buy back all of New York today and parts of Los Angeles as well ...

Another story you may have heard is about the inventor of chess. The emperor at that time, Sheram, was so happy about this invention that he wanted to grant the inventor, Zeta, any wish he wanted. The latter said that all he wanted as a reward was one grain of rice on the first square, two grains of rice on the second square, four grains of rice, eight and so on. As you know, the chessboard has 64 different squares. The emperor was then offended, as he found this request too simplistic and not appropriate to the gift of an emperor ... The rest is legend. Especially if we look at the numbers together: How much rice would the inventor have been entitled to in the end? The formula behind it is:

The power of the compound effect

Field64 = Field1 * 2^{64-1}

The result is the astronomical sum of over 9 trillion grains of rice. The colleagues of the TUM have calculated that this sum corresponds to almost 900 world annual harvests[3] (!). Unimaginable!

Why do I tell you these stories? Because you can use exactly this "power" also in your financial plans. Depending on how much you invest per month and how much starting capital you use, you can use the power.

Where do you encounter the interest rate in investments? In the stock market, in a bank account, in real estate purchases. In the case of value investments, you benefit primarily through the increases in value that are potentiated. For example, if your house increases in value by 1% every year, this will be calculated according to the interest-rate formula. Of course, the compound-effect can also play against you, for example with (high) loans. Sometimes this is unavoidable if you make high investments, for example in rented apartments or in your own house.

To make the compound-effect a little more transparent and thus easier to understand, I have created the following six tables for you. They show different percentages on the horizontal axis and the duration in years on the vertical axis downwards. In each case, the savings amount per month

---

[3] http://www-hm.ma.tum.de/ws1213/lba1/erg/erg07.pdf

and the starting capital varies. This allows you to quickly and easily read or estimate how much your investment could yield after a few years. Even if your desired sum is not exactly reflected in the table, you can still use the figures as a guide.

The applied formula looks like this:

$$Z = K \times q^t + \sum_{n=0}^{t-1} K_n \times q^n$$

$$= K \times q^t + K_n \times \frac{q^t - 1}{q - 1}$$

K is the starting capital, p (not shown here) is the assumed interest rate (for example, 0.04 for 4%), q = 1+p, t is the time in years (1,2,3 ...), n is the running variable of the summation formula into which (t-1) is substituted at the end.

The simplification here is that I assume that interest is applied only once a year and always to the entire sum of the year, even if savings are made monthly. This simplified assumption helps reduce what would otherwise be a much more complex formula.

The power of the compound effect

monthly 25 €; start investment 0 €		0%	2%	4%	6%	8%
Years	1	300 €	300 €	300 €	300 €	300 €
	2	600 €	606 €	612 €	618 €	624 €
	10	3,000 €	3,285 €	3,602 €	3,954 €	4,346 €
	15	4,500 €	5,188 €	6,007 €	6,963 €	8,146 €
	20	6,000 €	7,289 €	8,933 €	11,036 €	13,729 €
	25	7,500 €	9,609 €	12,494 €	16,459 €	21,932 €
	30	9,000 €	12,170 €	16,825 €	23,717 €	33,985 €

monthly 50 €; start investment 0 €		0%	2%	4%	6%	8%
Years	1	600 €	600 €	600 €	600 €	600 €
	2	1,200 €	1,212 €	1,224 €	1,236 €	1,248 €
	10	6,000 €	6,570 €	7,204 €	7,908 €	8,692 €
	15	9,000 €	10,376 €	12,014 €	13,966 €	16,291 €
	20	12,000 €	14,578 €	17,867 €	22,071 €	27,457 €
	25	15,000 €	19,218 €	24,988 €	32,919 €	43,864 €
	30	18,000 €	24,341 €	33,651 €	47,435 €	67,970 €

monthly 100 €; start investment 0 €		0%	2%	4%	6%	8%
Years	1	1,200 €	1,200 €	1,200 €	1,200 €	1,200 €
	2	2,400 €	2,424 €	2,448 €	2,472 €	2,496 €
	10	12,000 €	13,140 €	14,407 €	15,817 €	17,384 €
	15	18,000 €	20,752 €	24,028 €	27,931 €	32,583 €
	20	24,000 €	29,157 €	35,734 €	44,143 €	54,914 €
	25	30,000 €	38,436 €	49,975 €	65,837 €	87,727 €
	30	36,000 €	48,682 €	67,302 €	94,870 €	135,940 €

monthly 25 €; start investment 500 €		0%	2%	4%	6%	8%
Years	1	800 €	810 €	820 €	830 €	840 €
	2	1,100 €	1,126 €	1,153 €	1,180 €	1,207 €
	10	3,500 €	3,894 €	4,342 €	4,850 €	5,425 €
	15	5,000 €	5,861 €	6,908 €	8,181 €	9,732 €
	20	6,500 €	8,032 €	10,029 €	12,639 €	16,059 €
	25	8,000 €	10,429 €	13,827 €	18,605 €	25,356 €
	30	9,500 €	13,076 €	18,447 €	26,589 €	39,016 €

monthly 50 €; start investment 500 €		0%	2%	4%	6%	8%
Years	1	1,100 €	1,110 €	1,120 €	1,130 €	1,140 €
	2	1,700 €	1,732 €	1,765 €	1,798 €	1,831 €
	10	6,500 €	7,179 €	7,944 €	8,804 €	9,771 €
	15	9,500 €	11,049 €	12,915 €	15,164 €	17,877 €
	20	12,500 €	15,321 €	18,962 €	23,675 €	29,788 €
	25	15,500 €	20,038 €	26,320 €	35,065 €	47,288 €
	30	18,500 €	25,247 €	35,273 €	50,307 €	73,001 €

monthly 100 €; start investment 500 €		0%	2%	4%	6%	8%
Years	1	1,700 €	1,710 €	1,720 €	1,730 €	1,740 €
	2	2,900 €	2,944 €	2,989 €	3,034 €	3,079 €
	10	12,500 €	13,749 €	15,147 €	16,712 €	18,463 €
	15	18,500 €	21,425 €	24,929 €	29,129 €	34,169 €
	20	24,500 €	29,900 €	36,829 €	45,746 €	57,245 €
	25	30,500 €	39,257 €	51,308 €	67,983 €	91,151 €
	30	36,500 €	49,587 €	68,924 €	97,742 €	140,971 €

Based on the list above, it becomes visible that with a monthly investment of €100 and starting capital of €500, with the right investment strategy on the stock market (for example, via ETFs), with a profit of 8% on average, almost €30,000 will have accumulated after 20 years. In sum over 17,000 € profit compared to pure saving without interest is generated. After 40 years with this investment strategy over 300,000 € and after 60 years over 1,500,000 (!) € would be on your bank account. I have not even considered extra one-time payments or an increase of the 100 € monthly rate. Of course, 60 years is a long time, maybe you need a subset of the money for yourself and save the rest - that would be a compromise. Nowhere is it written that everyone must spend all their money, on the contrary, it makes sense to think about future generations as well, in the best case even grandchildren.

Saving recommendation for the parents of rich children

To achieve these figures, **I recommend investing 10% of your net income in long-term savings. In the best case, this should add up to more than €100 per month**. Subsequently, completely different sums are achievable. I started my investment career with 500 € per month and from each salary increase, from the Christmas bonus or similar, I immediately increased the sum by 10% or invested 10% of the one-time payment as well. This 10% is recommended in almost all well-known financial guidebooks, such as Bodo Schäfer, Ray Dalio or Tony Robbins. It is a sum on which one can or must be able to do without and thus "does not hurt". With this 10 % amount, a large amount of money is saved in the long run. The saved money is again iimmediately reinvested, for example in ETFs, shares or similar. You should also immediately put away 10% of any salary increase or one-time payments such as Christmas bonuses. You will see that this is much easier for you, as in the best case it is money that you have not yet fully budgeted for. This will make it easier for you to do without it.

It's almost a law of nature that no matter how much you earn, you will always manage to spend it all as your standard of living magically rises along with it. Or how do you explain the fact that when you were training or studying, you were also able to live well on a fraction of what you earn today? And yet you had too little money then, just as you do now, except that quite a few years and a few levels in the standard of living make a difference in between.

With this free play amount of money, you can then decide,

just like your child, which investment strategy to choose.

How do I do it? Since I often lack the time (and patience), I invest in ETFs, as explained several times now. When there are strong price fluctuations on the stock markets, I always have a smaller, four-digit sum in a call account to use to enter the market and make interesting deals. The last time was during the Corona crisis in March 2020, when all stock markets were in a tailspin.

If solid shares that have achieved good prices and paid out high dividends over decades, such as "Munich RE", suddenly move down by 30% points, one can already assume that these shares will also recover. Of course, the investors in Lehman Brothers, which went bankrupt in the last global economic crisis, thought the same thing.

As you can see, there is never absolute certainty. That's why a more detailed analysis is necessary, especially for individual stocks. In the next chapter, I will show you how you can carry out such an analysis based on a few key figures.

Excursus: Exchange Traded Funds – ETFs

You will see that I repeatedly talk about and recommend excursus Exchange Traded Funds - usually just called ETFs. Why? To summarize in a few words: because ETFs offer a simple, low-cost, and most importantly, no-maintenance investment strategy with good returns that are well-suited to beginners for these reasons.

Simple here means that if you invest in the DAX ETF, for example, you don't have to analyze and understand a single company, look at its annual reports to see exactly what the company plans to do and when. Instead, you invest in the entire index, so in the case of the DAX, you invest in 40 companies at once. The advantage, of course, is that you spread the risk and are not dependent on the decisions of individual companies.

Favorable means that - unlike equity funds - the management fees are virtually zero. This is a factor in your return/profit that should not be underestimated. If you have to give up 1% a year as a management fee in an actively managed fund (where a person/company actively buys and resells shares) and do not make a disproportionate profit, you will lose a lot of money in the long run (see also chapter "The power of the compound effect").

By **unmanaged**, I mean you don't have to check the ETF's balance every day. ETFs are long-term investments that are fed by a savings plan, which is a monthly deposit. I can only recommend selling ETFs in an absolute emergency. It should not happen if you have good financial planning.

Excursus: Exchange Traded Funds – ETFs

The biggest advantage of ETFs for me, however, is that they represent an entire market ("market" here means, for example, the German economy, i.e. the DAX) and it has been proven by countless financial experts and theories that it is impossible to beat the "market" in the long term, i.e. to be better than the DAX, for example. There are many reasons for this. The main reason is that an index like the DAX already tracks all undervalued and overvalued stocks, i.e. both cheap and expensive ones, and thus offers no opportunities for "bargains". The reason for that: the market already contains all available information, and thus the so-called secret tip no longer exists.

It should be noted here that you can of course find individual stocks that can yield a higher return than the DAX, but that is an exception and often means that you have to put a lot of time into analysis and research or simply be lucky. However, I am talking about "beating the market over the long term". You can read more about this topic at Gerd Kommer [6], among others.

Another reason, which cannot be measured, is our emotions. Emotions tempt us to act rashly, especially in stressful situations such as a price crash. We experience this especially with individual stocks and it often leads us to run after the broad masses when prices fall and sell as well. Most of the time, this ends in financial losses.

The same thing happens to fund managers, people we pay money to manage a portfolio. Despite all their experience, they too react emotionally to the stock market and can make

Excursus: Exchange Traded Funds – ETFs

mistakes as a result. Another disadvantage of trading individual stocks, in addition to the fees incurred. Of course, ETFs are also subject to price fluctuations and can also crash. However, since we already invest in ETFs with the principle of investing money for the long term, we do not sell during a crisis and thus do not lose money. Not even if the price falls below our original purchase price.

Stock valuation and investment strategies

In this book, I want to show your child (and you) the basics of investing and clarify its potential for your wealth. Therefore, I repeat again how important the first steps are and that you gain your first experience with (for now) a small amount of money. It is not crucial that you can already evaluate everything and every stock.

Nevertheless, you can increase the chance of a profitable stock purchase by performing a quick analysis based on a few key figures and thus classify the stock or the company. Some important metrics include:

1. The Return on Invest (ROI) = $\frac{Earnings}{Total\ capital}$
2. EBIT – Earnings before Interests and Taxes
3. Equity ratio = $\frac{Equity}{Total\ capital}$
4. Price earnings ratio (P/E ratio) = $\frac{Price\ of\ a\ share}{Profit\ of\ a\ share}$

Since there are some more relevant ratios, I wrote myself an Excel tool for the valuation of stocks, the so-called "Stock Valuation 1x1". The tool can be filled in semi-automatically based on stock market pages. Each ratio is weighted and evaluated according to the size of the number. Based on this, the tool gives a buy recommendation or not. The logic of the tool is based on the work of Mrs. Levermann, who has become the best broker in Germany with it several times.

Stock valuation and investment strategies

I will gladly provide you with this tool free of charge together with a manual on how to fill it. If you are interested, please just send me an email: **Goergantisch@gmail.com**

Ray Dalio, who created the largest fund in the world, takes a much more complex and apparently very successful approach, as his fund has "beaten the market", i.e. the benchmark Dow Jones stock index, in every year! His approach is based on analyzing "Big data" and looking for similarities in the market, world events and historical data. Dalio assumes that almost every condition has occurred in the past and had similar antecedents to the present or future. If his computer program recognizes these harbingers, it can adjust the fund accordingly, for example selling or buying shares. Unfortunately, you need at least 10 million euros to invest in that fund, so we must rely on simpler methods for now.

Due to the large number of possibilities to combine stocks, ETFs, commodities, rental properties, government bonds or products as a holistic portfolio, an investment strategy is needed. There are also guidelines for this as to what proportions of which positions should be combined. The idea behind this is to include different areas in one's portfolio that behave in opposite ways in times of crisis (one investment rises while another falls). This achieves a portfolio hedge. I will deal with this more complex topic in my second volume and for our purposes, it does not play a role yet.

If you are interested in further information: Please visit my website www.finanzen-kinderleicht.de. Unfortunately, as of yet, its only in German, but my presentation and coaching sessions are also offered in English. Feel free to reach out to me via the mentioned mail address.

The additional booster to get rich!

Unfortunately, we do not know each other personally, yet I believe we are very similar in at least one thing: We are optimizers. Optimizers of ourselves or we want to help others get the best out of themselves, especially those we love. Otherwise, you wouldn't have picked up the book and taken the time to learn more about finances for your child and yourself.

This character trait is what got me started investing back in the day because I didn't want to be mediocre anymore, and it also motivated me to write this book. I want to share my knowledge and I'm glad you bought it. However, getting rich is not just about money, it's also about discipline and being a good role model for your children.

So, I have a few more personal reminders for you on how you can take some optimization steps, not just financially:

1. Cancel your gym subscription if you no longer go. Less than 10% of all members go to the gym regularly. Even if you have a cheap contract and pay only €20 a month, that's €240 a year, €2,400 in ten years, and so on.
2. Fittingly, anything you don't do within 72 hours, you never do. You probably know this from opening letters or washing cars - which is very dirty right now ... be aware of this human weakness and always act immediately!
3. The so-called "PPP - Pain and Pleasure Principle" by Tony Robbins will help you to do this. He has worked out that our brain and thus our whole self knows only two motivators in life: less pain or more

pleasure. Any pleasure that happens to us, our brain wants to keep at all costs and minimize any pain. This also allows you to put every action to the test when you fail to do something again (see also point 2). Then your brain feels more pleasure not doing something than it does pain fearing you not doing it. This goes well until perhaps a deadline comes your way (for example, filing your taxes) and all of a sudden you do get it done quickly.
4. Write down your expenses and income and compare them. You'll be surprised and discover a "black hole" or two in your own balance sheet.
5. What are your fixed entertainment costs and what might you no longer need? (Netflix, Prime, Sky, Disney+ ...) That quickly adds up to over €100. Cancel the subscriptions and get rid of fixed costs you no longer need.
6. What the sports brand ASICS uses as a brand name is also a basis for you to be successful. ASICS stands for "Anima Sana in Corpore Sano" and means: a healthy soul in a healthy body. Exercise, nothing is better for relieving or avoiding frustration (or for thinking about money.)
7. If you are not doing well financially, you need to do something. Consider a small part-time job as it could help you temporarily, for example, delivering pizza on weekends. An extra €100 to €200 per month can make all the difference in helping you or giving you capital to invest.
8. People strive for spirituality and tranquility. This spirituality can be faith in God, it can be meditation or just simple rest. I am not in the situation to try to convert you with anything! I understand spirituality

The additional booster to get rich!

first and foremost as switching off - literally. This can mean reading a book early in the morning or late in the evening, a walk alone, prayer or meditation. Other people also find this in sports. See also point 6. All of this is important for you, try it, come down and you will see that it will help you. This is also proven by numerous studies. Personally, I do transcendental meditation, as do many successful businesspeople (including Jeff Bezos, Oprah Winfrey, Steve Jobs). Just Google it.

9. Observe yourself and your consumer behavior. During my work in the financial field with hundreds of adults, I have seen that almost everyone has a consumption weakness. By this I mean that you make a disproportionate number of purchases in one particular area. The classic item that men like to tease their wives with is, of course, the handbag that each woman seems to need 15 variations of. You will see, if it is not the handbag, that you also have such a weakness. For me, for example, it is shoes, sneakers, elegant shoes ... My parents buy two new jackets every year. Is that necessary? In most cases the answer is no. Check how much money you are literally sinking here and rather use at least a part of this sum for sustainable investing.

10. Get into action! No one has ever become rich from reading alone. The quickest way to do this is to be honest with yourself and formulate your wishes or your plight unsparingly, preferably in writing. Avoid weakening statements such as: "Others are doing worse". That may certainly be true. But for motivation, it helps you much more to compare yourself with people who are doing much better financially. Stay focused.

11. Don't listen to "well-intentioned" advice from people who aren't already where you want to be financially. If your neighbor tells you that ETFs won't work anyway, ask him where he gets that opinion, and don't let it influence you or drag you down. If he has no experience himself, he does not have the knowledge that you have acquired. Rather, talk to experienced people, listen to podcasts or read interesting biographies of really rich people.
12. Observe your state of mind depending on your food and alcohol consumption. If you can barely get out of bed every morning, either go to bed earlier or adjust your diet. Without energy, any "getting rich" will be difficult!
13. Get out of autopilot "this is how I've always done it" and into active role modeling for your child.

Conclusion for parents of rich kids

How many kids/teens do you know who know about banks, stock markets, or investing? Maybe you're like me and it's only a handful among thousands I've encountered myself or through my sons.

And how many of these children have stock accounts, a savings plan or a concrete monthly savings goal at the age of ten, twelve or 15? Certainly, even fewer ...

'It's not surprising, ask your friends and relatives who really knows about' finances. Probably not too many, since most have never been taught about finances as children or young adults.

When it comes to stock portfolios or other investments, I'm talking about portfolios or investments that your child follows and even grows with their own money. Of course, it's great if you made a savings plan for your child at birth, for example. In this way, you are supporting him or her on the path to becoming rich! You support it even more if you also put responsibility into the hands of the child, and this happens through active participation.

This book can be a foundation for your child's financial knowledge and thus "getting rich". By applying the knowledge, your child can stand out a lot from other children and adults. In doing so, you are giving your child a valuable head start on the marathon of life and ultimately that is what all parents want for their children. A good/better future and, "for them to have it easier than you do, without you doing all the work for them".

Conclusion for parents of rich kids

I hope this book will impart the important financial knowledge to your child and that you are now well equipped to guide your child in the process. Good luck in getting rich!

Finanzen kinderleicht
Coaching.Investmentstrategien.Vorsorge

 You want more information on investing? or more free tools?

 Take a look at my website: www.finanzen-kinderleicht.de

 Here you can download free financial assessment tools or sign up for my newsletter.

 Any questions? Feel free to write me, I will answer every e-mail
goergantisch@gmail.com

Note for my English readers: the website is in German, I offer every service in English as well

Appendix

Word Explanations

I will explain useful words that can be used in getting rich. I also explain words or phrases that do not appear in the book. This also helps when reading other books.

Word	Explanation
Share	For the buyer of the share, i.e. the shareholder, a share means that it gives him rights in the company. The goal of the buyer is to make money with his share, for example through price increases or a dividend. The seller, i.e. the company, wants to make money by selling the share to the shareholder in order to invest it in the further development of the company.
Shareholder	„owner of a share (see

Word Explanations

	above).
Dividend	Share of the company's profit that a company pays to its shareholders.
Buy and hold	Refers to a strategy for dealing with shares. It means: one buys a share and does not sell it again. In doing so, it is important to receive (high) dividends and thus generate a profit for oneself.
Stock exchange	Refers to the trading place where shares are bought and sold. Today, the stock exchange is mostly virtual for the shareholder on the PC or cell phone, i.e. online.
Bank	In connection with money, a bank is an institution that manages and lends money.
Share price	Share price describes the current value of a share. This can be tracked on the

	stock exchange, for example online. The share price is essentially determined by supply and demand.
ETF	Exchange Traded Funds – e.g. the DAX
Portfolio	Describes, in terms of money, the composition of different investments. A portfolio can be, for example, various shares (Apple, BMW, Nintendo ...) but also a combination of shares with houses or other valuable investments.
Interestes	Amount of money that customers have to pay to a bank from which they have borrowed money. Also: an amount of money that customers get when they have invested money.

Word Explanations

Investment strategy	A predetermined goal at which time people who want to get rich will invest how much in which stock or product.
DAX	German stock index consisting of 40 companies and thus 40 individual shares.
EBIT	Earnings before Interests and Taxes. This value is a typical key figure used to value companies on the stock exchange.
ROI	Return on Invest – Return on investment, i.e. how much money do I get out of what I put in?
Investition	Money investment or object in which someone "puts" their money with the goal of getting more money out.

Book recommendations

I have read countless textbooks over the last 20 years and many of them more than once which I hope affirms the phrase, "Man is the sum of all the books he has ever read." There must be some truth to this, because by reading in a few hours and hundreds of pages, we can all share in the experience of countless people with similar questions and problems. Therefore, I would like to recommend some of my favorites related to finance and personal development.

Finance

- [1] Robert Kyosaki – Rich dad, poor dad
- [2] André Kostolany – Die Kunst über Geld nachzudenken
- [3] Sam Walton – Made in Amerika
- [4] Warren Buffet – Sein Weg. Seine Methode. Seine Strategie.
- [5] Tony Robbins – Money
- [6] Gerd Kommer – Souverän Investieren mit Indexfonds und ETFs
- [7] Gerd Kommer – Immobilienfinanzierung für Selbstnutzer
- [8] Napoleon Hill – Think and grow rich

Book recommendations

- [9] Bodo Schäfer – Der Weg zur finanziellen Freiheit
- [10] Ray Dalio – Principles
- [11] Susan Levermann – Der entspannte Weg zum Reichtum

Personality Development

- [12] Dale Carnegie – Wie man Freunde gewinnt
- [13] Tony Robbins – Awaken the Giant within
- [14] Tony Robbins – Grenzenlose Energie
- [15] Alexander Hartmann – Mit dem Elefant durch die Wand
- [16] Michael Winterhoff – Lasst Kinder wieder Kinder sein
- [17] Samy Molcho – Körpersprache des Erfolgs
- [18] Bodo Schäfer – Die Gesetze der Gewinner
- [19] Thorsten Havener – Ich weiß was du denkst
- [20] Thorsten Havener – Ohne Worte, was andere über dich denken
- [21] Thorsten Havener – Denk doch was du willst
- [22] Jack Nasher – Deal

Summary of the book

Most people don't like to read a book twice. I, too, am one of them. However, I have started to summarize the books I read in my journal. This allows me to quickly reread in a quiet minute what messages were important to me in the book. I always do this during summer vacation and over Christmas, summarizing several books I read during the year. This way, I have at least two longer periods of time during the year when I only focus on the topic of continuing education. Perhaps this is also an idea for you and your child, as this method can solidify ideas more than reading books only once.

Hereby, I would like to make this task easier for you and your child by putting together the key messages of my book. This way you have everything together in a condensed form and can go back to the page and read the context of these highlighted intermediate summaries.

Summary of the book

What do you need money for?

What money actually is ...

Money is first and foremost a means of feeling secure and not having to worry about money. Thus, it can help us not to be unhappy. Money does not make us happy alone, there are many other things like happiness, love and health.

→ On the topic: Does money make you happy or not?

♠Intermediate conclusion♠

So you see: without money, shopping would either be very costly (bringing lots of eggs to barter) or not possible at all (when our barter goods are not needed).

→ About: why money is above all also practical for not having to barter

♩Summarized♩

Money is a means to an end and facilitates

the trading of goods, food, or greater. It is its own agreement, so it is a different way of trading than bartering, for example.

So why is money important today?

!That means!

Today you can buy things with money. Your parents don't use their labor to grow fruits or vegetables to feed themselves and you. They can hardly do that anymore. Instead, they offer their labor to a company and get money for it.

➔ In context, why is it good that there is money?

Why do people want more money?

♥ To become rich ...

Because of the desire to be better than

Summary of the book

others, most people want to get rich! That's a strong drive. For you too?

→ Here I explained what drives people, which is to outdo others.

▶ The exercises ◀

Please don't just skip the exercises. No one has ever gotten rich from just reading. The important thing is that you internalize what you read, and the easiest way to do that is through these short exercises. You can always return to the exercises if something occurs to you in between ... Ask your parents what they would write here!

What does being rich mean to you?

•Conclusion•

You can see from the different answers, "being rich" can also refer to many other things than just money, for example, happiness and health. (In the next chapters, however, we will focus on money and everything that can be grasped with the hands when we talk about being rich. Of course, we won't forget happiness and health.)

→ About: Different interpretations of "being rich." So being rich is also a feeling.

Saving - Start early and get rich faster!

▶ What have you learned?

1. Saving is especially important when you are doing well. However, saving does not always refer to money only, as we have seen. It is also possible to save on food.
2. It's important to plan ahead. This was not only true in 1723, it is still true today.
3. You must not waste anything, neither food nor money. Otherwise, it will take its revenge at some point.

→ The summary from the story with Marie, why it pays to save.

Summary of the book

▶ What can you do concretely now?

First of all, you should be aware that everyone has this weakness to save and provide for the future.

Secondly, you can make a more conscious decision to save now.

Third, you should have a goal that you want to save for. To help you, you can answer the following questions and fill in your answers below ...

→ People often find it difficult to plan for an abstract and distant future, so we also find it difficult to save

▶ What is my recommendation?

I recommend that you put away 25% of your allowance and money gifts (birthday, Christmas, and so on) for a specific savings goal, preferably one from the list on the previous page.

Another 25% you should save away and not spend at all. This is the foundation for getting rich and will be invested later!

Summary of the book

➔ Related to the picture below, what percentages of money should you put aside.

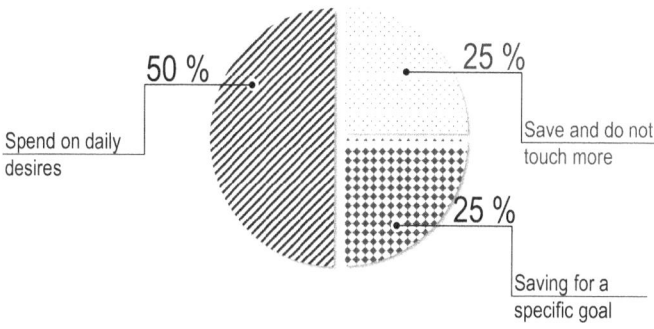

50 % — Spend on daily desires
25 % — Save and do not touch more
25 % — Saving for a specific goal

Pocket money calculator

Last year	single	Extrapolated for one year	product
Pocket money (per week)	€	x 52	€
or			
Pocket money (per month)	€	x 12	€
Birthday money	€	x 1	€
Christmas/Easter or other (religious) festivals	€	x 1	€
Other money	€	x 1	€
Other money	€	x 1	€
Sum (Attention: of course you can add the pocket money only once)			€

Summary of the book

▶ What are you learning by saving?

- To plan for the future by thinking about what you want to own or buy someday.
- To be conscientious with money.
- To save for the sake of saving itself and gain a sense that you can get by with less money. This is very important, it limits the compulsive desire for "more".

And by the way, you take your first steps to becoming rich.

Investments - how to get more with less!

▶ What have you learned?

- If you work hard for something and invest time, it's worth it. And most of the time, you eventually get something back (almost for free).
- Sometimes you work hard for a long time for something in the here and now without any visible result.

The future result is all the greater for it! An apple tree, for example, takes almost ten years to bear apples that can be harvested.
- Community helps not only in weeding, but also in investing and investing money, because you can share the work (the so-called invest or your search results).
- It's always wise to ask experienced people, such as your grandparents or your parents, for advice. This way you can avoid making the same mistakes that thousands of people have made before you.
- Good things sometimes take a little bit longer, and other times I can take generations as in the example of Helena and Isabel. A generation lasts about 30 years. Between Isabel and Helena there are even more than two generations, namely 70 years.

➔ As a summary for the story with the orchard

Summary of the book

These investments exist

Investing or "investing" money means that someone gives his money to the bank. The bank works with it, lends it on, for example, and after a year gets **more** money back as a thank you. The "more money" is also called interest

"Borrowing" means someone does not have enough money himself and asks the bank to give him a sum (lend). After, for example, one year you have to pay back the money + a fee for borrowing

Summary of the book

→ The summary of how a bank works.

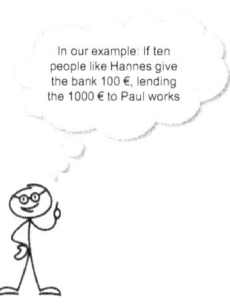

The balance sheet of a bank

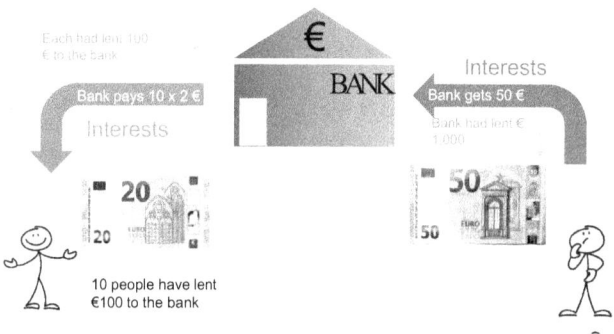

Summary of the book

Conclusion ♪

Borrowing money is sometimes necessary, as with Paul in our example. Also, when you need very large amounts of money because you want to build a house, for example, adults borrow money. Most of the time, however, borrowing money and paying interest is not good, especially for smaller amounts of money for things you don't really need, like the newest TV when the old one still works. Those who borrow money often pay interest spread over several months, which then add up to a lot of money and prevent you from actually saving for the whole year! Therefore, better save the money for such a purchase. And beforehand.

→ About banks and borrow money and the necessary interest.

Investments in products: Supply and demand

Rule of thumb♠

As a rule of thumb, you can remember: few or rare products with high demand (that is, something that many people want) mean high prices.

Figure: DAX trend in points over years, significant increase visible in ten years.

Summary of the book

What do you learn from it?

1. Supply and demand determine the price, also on the stock exchange.
2. Try to always classify where you stand (price high or low?) before you buy something.
    a. This can be done by simply thinking.
    b. You can also analyze the stock market and look at the stock trends.
    c. There are various ratios and websites for this. I recommend the book by Susanne Levermann "The relaxed way to wealth". You should read it together with your parents, because it contains a lot of technical terms.
3. The stock market is very complex.
4. You can win a lot of money in the stock market, but you can also lose it. If it were otherwise, all people would be rich.
5. All stock investors try to buy at a cheap price and sell at a more expensive price. Yet it's not always clear exactly what cheap means.
6. Companies you buy can also go bankrupt. This means that you, as an investor, lose a large part of your money. This is what distinguishes a share from a product, such as your LEGO excavator. Because you still own it, regardless of whether LEGO goes bankrupt or not.

Summary of the book

My steps to wealth

13 concrete steps what you can do now to become rich:

1. You need money that you can invest: Make a savings plan together with your parents.
    a. As a reminder, use 50% to play and have fun and save the other 50%. Here's my recommendation: save 25% on something you want to buy and use the remaining 25% to invest.
2. If you don't have enough money or you want to get rich even faster: Think about how you can earn more money. Maybe you can help your neighbors, you will surely think of something (this also applies to adults, they can for example look for a small side job if the actual earnings are not enough to invest).
3. Find out about products you want to invest in. LEGO is just one example. Note here: The more a product interests you personally, the easier it will be to trade it. If LEGO doesn't interest you, think about what else is out there. Rare comics, old Barbie dolls or something completely different ...
4. Only invest money that you don't need. If you lose it, it's bad, but it won't cause you financial hardship.
5. Look at every gain, but also every loss, as a lesson of life. Don't be sad about it, just do better next time. You will learn even more from the defeats than from the easy victories, because the defeats hurt you.
6. Read a lot of books. Why? Because reading educates and in a very short time you can experience and eventually learn the knowledge of decades of successful and exciting personalities. Besides, reading stimulates your brain to think

(along). And is therefore very valuable. Especially if you want to become rich. Thereby you can read all kinds of books ...
- a. Books about money/investments
- b. Novels - nothing better than exercising your imagination, even when it comes to investing.
- c. Non-fiction books about whatever interests you (horses, the environment, ships...) This will allow you to deepen your knowledge in a specialized field and who knows, maybe it will be of some use to you when investing. Most of all, it should be fun for you.
- d. Books about rich, famous, interesting people: biographies. It's a very easy way to broaden your horizons and get opinions and ideas about things you might not have even thought about before.

    Many successful people will tell you, "You are the sum of the books you read."

7. Learn from your friends and your parents how to get rich or how not to get rich. Negative examples are important, too.
8. Talk to your parents about money and finances and have them explain anything you don't understand.
9. Discuss with your parents whether you can open a savings account at a bank into which you can deposit money every month.
10. For the brave, consider with your parents whether you also want to set up an account for investing. I recommend simple "trader accounts" here, such as at Consorsbank. The fees are very low. I describe everything else about this especially for your parents in their part of this book.

Summary of the book

11. Ask yourself the right questions such as: what do I have to do to become rich? You will see, your brain will magically suggest answers.
12. Never think: I can't afford that! That blocks you from your goal to become rich. The question should be: How can I afford this?
13. Don't let others tell you what is possible and what is not. And above all, evaluate whether that person is an expert in that particular field, or just has an opinion on the subject. You wouldn't ask Lionel Messi how a rocket works or a bank employee how to shoot the best free kick. Check whether someone is really helping you with their views or just trying to discourage you.

Summary of the book

The magic for my wealth

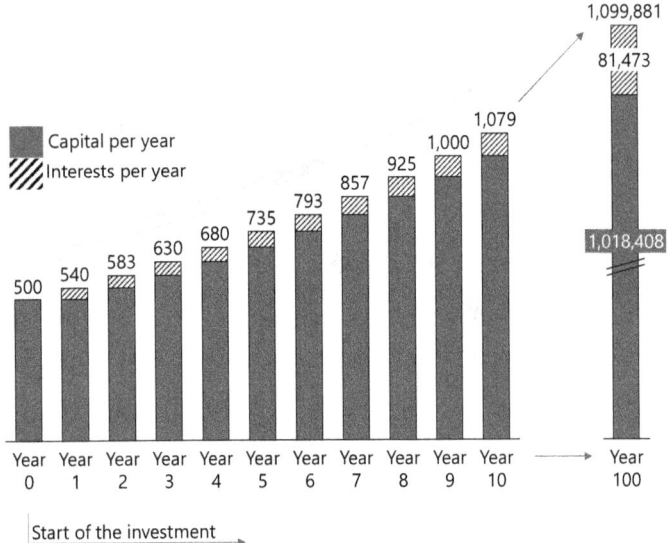

Summary of the book

Timeplan of getting rich

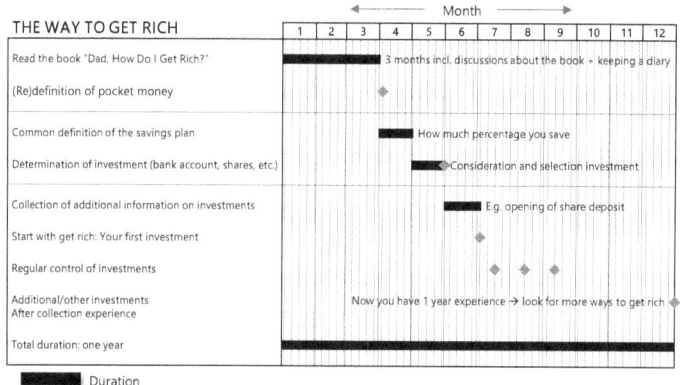

From here begins Part II of the book - "For all parents of rich children".

Introduction for Parents: How to use the book effectively

Since this is not a novel or a classic children's book, I ask you to observe how strongly your child is motivated to read the book by himself. Of course, the ideal case is that he reads through the book by himself. However, if it is not so motivated, here are some ideas of what you can do to help it read:

1. If your child is not self-motivated to read the book, read the book aloud and tell matching stories from their own life. Your child will find it exciting to hear examples from mom or dad from their youth.
2. Don't force the book on your child, use quiet, relaxed moments (perhaps the summer vacation together) to introduce the book to your child.
3. You know your child best and know what and how to motivate him or her most effectively. Here, people like to distinguish between two basic types: People who are motivated "toward something," such as getting rich. Then there is the type of person who is motivated "away from something," that is, by an avoidance. For example, by avoiding being "poor." While this sounds similar, it is completely different for those the motivational approach. Both for you and for your child. What is it like for your child? Pay attention and, if you're not sure, test different approaches to motivation.

4. Create an incentive for reading and working through the book, such as visiting the zoo, going to the movies, or going swimming together. Be a good motivator.
5. Take notes while reading and encourage your child to do the same. No one has ever gotten rich from reading alone, but only from the actions that follow. And, this implementation will be easier for you and your child if you can write down ideas, concepts or concrete actions in your own words and then take them to hand again and again. You will see that this is more efficient, and above all more effective, than looking up certain things again and again in a book. It is always your own words and thoughts that are best remembered. Besides, what you have noted down once sticks better in your memory. I therefore recommend keeping an excellence diary. More on this later in the text and in the last chapter.
6. I have included simple exercises and reflections. Feel free to do these together with your child and also think about what you would write in. Then you can compare. Your child will probably find it quite exciting to see what mom or dad's goals, dreams, or wishes are.
7. At the end of the book, you will find a schedule for one year with concrete suggestions for you and your child to implement. It is best to work through this after you have read the book.
8. Surely your child will also be motivated by the prospect of investing 100€ together with you at the end.

Basically, this book is nothing but one of the most important homework assignments your child will do. As a father of two, academic achievement and all subjects of learning are hugely important to me. However, for "real life", binomial

Summary of the book

formulas or the exact date when the French Revolution took place or how van Gogh executed his brush strokes are often not that crucial. That's why I feel it's important to add this book on finance to the broad base of school knowledge, providing a parallel, school-based education for real life.

What can you do for your rich child!?

▶ Why pocket money?

- It is first contact with money, with it one learns: What is a lot, what is little money? Your child recognizes this when he or she sees how much one can afford or not afford with 5 € per month.
- It can create the motivation to earn more on their own.
- This can lead to children being proud of being able to afford something themselves.

➔ Reminder why it makes sense to pay pocket money, no matter how poor or rich you feel.

Summary of the book

Age of the child	Recommended pocket money (Youth Welfare Office)	My recommendation (Variable part in %)	My recommendation (without variable part in €, rounded)
4-5 years	0.5 € / week	- 0 %	0.5 € / week
6-7 years	1.5 – 2 € / week	- 10…20 %	1.2 – 1.8 € / week
8-9 years	2 – 3 € / week	- 10…20 %	1.6 – 2.7 € / week
10-11 years	13 – 16 € / month	- 20 %	10 – 13 € / month
12-13 years	18 – 22 € / month	- 20 %	14 – 18 € / month
14-15 years	25 – 30 € / month	- 20 %	20 – 24 € / month
16-17 years	35 – 45 € / month	- 30 %	25 – 30 € / month
18 years	70 € / month		Dependent on own job[1]

[1] 30 € basic pocket money; pay more pocket money only if own money is also earned (maximum: 50 €)

➔ Overview of the youth welfare office on the amount of pocket money

▶ **Reasons for having a savings account.**
- Learning how to handle savings/money
- Getting to know banks
- Realizing how time and saving can work wonders.
- Taking responsibility
- Learning independence in dealing with money
- Setting savings goals (together with you)

And just as important...

Summary of the book

▶ Reasons for a Trader account
- First contact with shares/ETF
- Thereby understanding the stock market
- Learning to deal with and endure loss in the stock market as well.
- Achieve first profits!

The power of the compound effect

monthly 25 €; start investment 0 €	0%	2%	4%	6%	8%
Years 1	300 €	300 €	300 €	300 €	300 €
2	600 €	606 €	612 €	618 €	624 €
10	3,000 €	3,285 €	3,602 €	3,954 €	4,346 €
15	4,500 €	5,188 €	6,007 €	6,983 €	8,146 €
20	6,000 €	7,289 €	8,933 €	11,036 €	13,729 €
25	7,500 €	9,609 €	12,494 €	16,459 €	21,932 €
30	9,000 €	12,170 €	16,825 €	23,717 €	33,985 €

monthly 50 €; start investment 0 €	0%	2%	4%	6%	8%
Years 1	600 €	600 €	600 €	600 €	600 €
2	1,200 €	1,212 €	1,224 €	1,236 €	1,248 €
10	6,000 €	6,570 €	7,204 €	7,908 €	8,692 €
15	9,000 €	10,376 €	12,014 €	13,966 €	16,291 €
20	12,000 €	14,578 €	17,867 €	22,071 €	27,457 €
25	15,000 €	19,218 €	24,988 €	32,919 €	43,864 €
30	18,000 €	24,341 €	33,651 €	47,435 €	67,970 €

monthly 100 €; start investment 0 €	0%	2%	4%	6%	8%
Years 1	1,200 €	1,200 €	1,200 €	1,200 €	1,200 €
2	2,400 €	2,424 €	2,448 €	2,472 €	2,496 €
10	12,000 €	13,140 €	14,407 €	15,817 €	17,384 €
15	18,000 €	20,752 €	24,028 €	27,931 €	32,583 €
20	24,000 €	29,157 €	35,734 €	44,143 €	54,914 €
25	30,000 €	38,436 €	49,975 €	65,837 €	87,727 €
30	36,000 €	48,682 €	67,302 €	94,870 €	135,940 €

monthly 25 €; start investment 500 €	0%	2%	4%	6%	8%
1	800 €	810 €	820 €	830 €	840 €
2	1,100 €	1,126 €	1,153 €	1,180 €	1,207 €
10	3,500 €	3,894 €	4,342 €	4,850 €	5,425 €
15	5,000 €	5,861 €	6,908 €	8,181 €	9,732 €
20	6,500 €	8,032 €	10,029 €	12,639 €	16,059 €
25	8,000 €	10,429 €	13,827 €	18,605 €	25,356 €
30	9,500 €	13,076 €	18,447 €	26,589 €	39,016 €

monthly 50 €; start investment 500 €	0%	2%	4%	6%	8%
1	1,100 €	1,110 €	1,120 €	1,130 €	1,140 €
2	1,700 €	1,732 €	1,765 €	1,798 €	1,831 €
10	6,500 €	7,179 €	7,944 €	8,804 €	9,771 €
15	9,500 €	11,049 €	12,915 €	15,164 €	17,877 €
20	12,500 €	15,321 €	18,962 €	23,675 €	29,788 €
25	15,500 €	20,038 €	26,320 €	35,065 €	47,288 €
30	18,500 €	25,247 €	35,273 €	50,307 €	73,001 €

monthly 100 €; start investment 500 €	0%	2%	4%	6%	8%
1	1,700 €	1,710 €	1,720 €	1,730 €	1,740 €
2	2,900 €	2,944 €	2,989 €	3,034 €	3,079 €
10	12,500 €	13,749 €	15,147 €	16,712 €	18,463 €
15	18,500 €	21,425 €	24,929 €	29,129 €	34,169 €
20	24,500 €	29,900 €	36,829 €	45,746 €	57,245 €
25	30,500 €	39,257 €	51,308 €	67,983 €	91,151 €
30	36,500 €	49,587 €	68,924 €	97,742 €	140,971 €

Representation of simple calculations to the orientation with how much investments becomes with compound-effect how much money.

The table serves as a quick orientation.

My excellence diary

The Excellence Diary is designed to help you and your parents record both good and bad things about finances. Making a mistake is not bad, but making the same mistake twice is annoying. That's why you can record both great successes and mistakes here. By reading it regularly, you can always keep it in mind. At Amazon you can find a cheap excellence diary, suitable for this book, which I have created for you. If you feel like (I highly recommend) keeping a diary regularly, buy a real diary.

Date:

Your text

Date:

Dein Text

Date:

Date:

My excellence diary

Date:

Date:

Date:

Date:

My excellence diary

Date:

Date:

Date:

Date:

Date:

My excellence diary

Date:

Date:

Date:

Date:

My excellence diary

Date:

Date:

Date:

Date:

Date:

My excellence diary

Date:

Date:

Date:

Date:

My excellence diary

Date:

Date:

www.ingramcontent.com/pod-product-compliance
Lightning Source LLC
Chambersburg PA
CBHW071409210526
45465CB00001B/307